Breathing Under Water

Photo by Jo Bellonci

by Susan Bright
and friends

Plain View Press
P. O.42255
Austin, TX 78704

plainviewpress.net
sbright1@austin.rr.com
1-512-441-2452

Copyright Susan Bright, 2001. All rights reserved.
ISBN: 1-891386-17-4
Library of Congress Number: 00-192965

Cover art, "Breathing Under Water," acrylic and sculpted clay, by Brian Michael Pion, © 2000.

Copyright for photos within reverts to the artists.

*Dedicated to Beverly Stephen Sheffield
March 7, 1913 – December 10, 1999*

Photo by Lois Sheffield, taken the day the Sheffield
Hillside Theater was dedicated to Bev, March 7, 1998.

A Lap for Beverly

I did a lap today for Beverly who isn't able to come
to the water where he would rather be than anyplace
except possibly someplace with Lois quiet,
where they can read, or talk.

I did a lap today for Beverly who is everyone's
Barton Springs hero for a thousand reasons,
one of my personal heroes.

He tells me poems, recites them by heart.
I say, *Where did that come from?*
because I read a fair amount of poetry and I like
his poems but I don't know them,

because he is a good man, one of the best.
He says, *I don't know.*

I think he makes them up.
He gave me a story about Rags.
He gave me poems he wanted to have read for him,
sometime, he said, but not yet, because he's in rehab,
walking so he can make it back to swim.

I did a lap for Beverly today, the second one,
the one I sometimes convince myself
not to finish, if it's too cold, or if I'm tired.

He said when he was my age he decided to get in shape.
So I thought I might try it too.
He started keeping track of his distance, swam
to Los Angeles, then set out to sea.

We figured he'd gone further than Ben
who swam across the Atlantic Ocean.

Today I did an extra lap for Beverly, who says
every time he gets in our cold water in the winter,
You have to be a damn fool to do this. And we are.

And we think of that, just before we get in,
when we know it's going to be cold, and it is. It's cold.
And we are damn fools. And better for it.

Today, I did a lap for Beverly because every time
I see him, no exceptions, I am better, stronger —
touched by that cold emerald grace we have him,
as much as anyone, to thank for.

Contents

A Lap for Beverly	3
Introduction	7
Breathing Under Water	10
. . . and friends	11
Swimming in Hope	13
Swimming to Greenwich	14
Bonding to the Creek	15
Cormorant	16
Swimming in Apples	17
Twilight	18
Crows, Blackbirds, Black Suits	19
Finding Becky	20
Lappers	21
I Turn into a Fish	23
Soup	24
Catch of the Day	25
Things That Weren't Lost	26
Riding the Currents	27
Cat Napping at the Pool	28
The Swimming Angel	29
Swimming Back to Our Senses	30
Egg	31
Riddle of the River	32
Swimming in Socks	34
Getting Organized	35
Diving off the Hancock Center	36
Save	38
Swimming in the Shallows	39
Unraveling	40
Coming Up For Air	41
Perspective	42
Swimming in Negation	43
What the River Knows	44
Blue Jewel	45
Often I swim in air —	46
Inside the Pineapple	47
That Which Connects	49
Swimming God	50

Winter Swimming	51
The Universal Deck Change	52
Sweep	53
How to Swim in a Fjord	54
Jugging	55
The Final Drift	56
About to be a Whole Lot Better	58
Swimming Together	59
The Garden in the River	61
Swimming in Regret	62
Floating in Traffic	64
Swimming in Karma	65
I Like to Think of Father	67
Everything Wrong and Broken	68
A Question of Degree	69
Emerald	70
Drowning in Teachers	71
Swimming in Flowers	72
A Thick Layer of Time	74
Swimming in Grief	76
Eclipse Party	77
Elephant Buddha	78
Swimming in Hearings	79
I know how to swim in moonlight alone	80
The River Needs a Friend	81
Swimming with Rick	82
Bodycount	84
Myth of Proportion	85
Urban Drift	86
Swimming in the Beginning	88
Iris	89
Swimming in Choice	90
Going Back for More	93
About the Poet	95
About the Artist	95

Introduction

What follows is a cycle of poems about swimming threaded from my own voice and the voices of people I know. Beverly Sheffield gave me the idea. It is poetry in which the voices of a community are woven into the voice of the poet. The central metaphor is water and the primary setting is Barton Springs, a beautiful spring fed swimming pool in Austin, Texas.

There is drift in these poems. They flow the way we do, sometimes off a cliff, sometimes gently around the bend. I've let the metaphor go where it will, from water to space to community. When I showed the poems to one of my swimming friends, Armin Remesat, he said they were a labor of enchantment. Perhaps they are.

In the winter of 1998, I was out of the water a fair amount of the time between December and April. Any outdoor swimmer can tell you, if you are out more than five days in the winter, good luck getting back in until spring. I'd been out of touch with my swimming friends. So it didn't occur to me that not seeing Bev was a problem until one day in April I discovered he'd been gravely ill.

I sat on the shallow end steps. It was a gray and balmy afternoon. I'd been out too long. Events had traumatized me to the max and I was exhausted. I needed to swim. I knew if I got in the water I would swim. The wind blew velvet and insistent against my reticence and I thought of Beverly. It was terrible he couldn't swim. So I got in. I did a lap for him. When I got home I wrote A *Lap for Beverly*.

I left copies at the gate for the regulars and sent a copy to Bev and Lois. Lois called to say Bev loved the poem. A week or so later Bev called himself. I wasn't sure I'd get to talk to him again. It made me profoundly happy to be allowed to do so.

I tacked the poem to the pool bulletin board. Pretty soon Helen Besse organized a sign up sheet so everybody could keep track of their laps and *give* them to Bev. He loved it.

One day, again after I'd been out of the water too long, I was surprised to see the poem was gone. I geared up, was about to get in the water, glanced up and the poem was posted again. I heard someone talking about Beverly so I asked how he was. The man, Ron Davis, told me Beverly was slightly better, that someone had written a lovely poem about him. Ron said he had taken it down and made copies. I told him I was the poet. He liked that. I liked it too. It seemed to me that the poem had work to do, that it belonged to the community.

Then it occurred to me that to write in the voice of that community would be an artistically interesting project. Thus commenced one of the most joyful writing journeys I've undertaken. I carried the metaphor as I traveled, adding the voices of the people I care about, new friends, old ones to the mix.

Beverly Sheffield was a swimmer. He was also, we later discovered, Austin's version of Benjamin Franklin. He was a founder or board member for many of our civic institutions. He convinced the City Council to give park space to Isamu Taniguchi who created the Zilker Hillside Japanese Garden which is dedicated to the memory of the people who died at Hiroshima and to World Peace.

It was Beverly's idea to string a spiral of colored lights from the Moonlight Tower in Zilker Park, providing Austin with the dizziest Christmas Tree in America, and one of the most beautiful. The amphitheater in Zilker Park is named after Bev, its founder. He started the Austin Community Foundation and persuaded people to fund it.

Swimmers mostly knew him as one of our more delightful companions, athletic, the embodiment of what Barton Springs meant to us and to Austin. After he died, we were amazed to read about all of his accomplishments. Bev never bragged. But he did live for community, and he provided the inspiration from which this collection of poetry evolved.

I first thought to footnote the speakers in each poem but that grew repetitious, so I have compiled a list of people whose voices I've woven into the poems. I've tried to get names spelled correctly. Sometimes I've changed a name and sometimes I invent. I'm not trying to invade anyone's privacy. I often quote Sharon Olds who said about poetry written in the first person, *It is not important that it be biographical. It is important that it be true.* I've told people who have shared their thoughts about water that I'll weave something of what they tell me into a poem. I tell them, *If you don't like what I've said, I probably won't change it, but I'll take out your name.*

I haven't tried to say the names of everyone who has worked to protect the water here or to list all the regular swimmers, rather I have written about people I see at the pool and the ones who have talked to me about it. I didn't send out a call for stories. I wanted the process to flow from the community as I experienced it.

Andrew Wyeth used to request approval of his portraits from the people he painted. Most artists don't. I like the idea because these people aren't objects of art, they are my friends. I've tried to show the poems to the people whose words and spirits are woven into them. There are many shining beings here, incredible people who swim in this water, who understand what Beverly always said, *Barton Springs is more a state than a place*.

In the obituary for Bev, the family wrote about what I have come to think of as the spirit of this book.

. . . high on his list (of awards) must have been Bev's Swim to Hawaii. This is how it happened: Bev decided to become a serious swimmer at the age of 50. Most recently, he decided to swim in Barton Springs the distance between New York city and Los Angeles. From a marked spot on a curb at the Springs to the dam and back is one-fourth mile. Thus, he measured his trip of 2,820 miles. Completed, he determined to "swim" to Hawaii, and was 541 miles into the Pacific ocean when ill health stopped him. Inspired by a poem written by Susan Bright and organized by Helen Besse, some 50 fellow swimmers swam 2,820 miles in approximately 2,250 swims to complete the trek.

Barton Springs is what has kept me in Austin, at first because of the magnificent emerald water and eventually because of the community. When my son was small our street wasn't safe for children, so the pool became our neighborhood. Dan Morris said when he first started swimming here, he would look at the people gathered beneath the old pecan tree across from the diving board. They were the regulars. *Now*, he said, *we're them*. Eventually our children will be the regulars, or someone else will, that is if we manage to protect this place where, as indigenous people thought, Rainbow cracked Stone and Water was born.

One of the first poems I ever wrote, and the first title I envisioned for a book was **Breathing Under Water**. The poem has never been published and I've never used it as a book title—until now.

Susan Bright
11/4/00

Breathing Under Water

*You know
how sometimes someone
dreams of
breathing under water
and with age old
power
dives for clarity?*

Jo Bellonci with Francisco Barrientos his first summer at the pool.
Photo by Ingrid Gabríel.

. . . and friends

Thanks to Glee Ingram for editing still another collection of my poetry. She has the next to the last word about how my poetry appears. Thanks also to Sarah Bolz for editing and proof reading and for the work she does for Plain View Press. Thanks to Jo Bellonci for proof reading, taking pictures underwater and for helping me get names straight. I apologize in advance to anyone whose name is wrong. Barton Springs swimmers are notorious for not knowing each other's names (and not recognizing each other with clothes on). Thanks to Francisco and Esmeralda, Willow, Isabel and all the babies who remind me it's all right to be human. Thanks to Scott Lackey for keeping an office copy of the manuscript so people could see *their* poems develop. Thanks to Scott Greer for some great emails from Spain. Thanks to Brian Pion for creative energy, vision and for the cover art. As always I thank John C. Andrews and Daryl Bright Andrews for managing to nurture and live in my world of books. Thanks particularly to Daryl for providing me with amazing opportunities for growth and to both him and his brother, Nick, for their courage and love. Thanks to Anne and Megan Bright for the opportunity to traverse the Golden Gate Bridge. Thanks to Helen Bryant for showing me how to be an artist.

And thanks to the following people who have shared thoughts, words, swimming style and spirit with me as I explored the rich and powerful voice of a community.

Alice Embree, Alicia Davida, Alyce Guynn, Amiten Rose, Ann Greer, Anna Geismar, Anne S. Bright, Annette Morris, Armin Remesat, Arye Shapiro, Barbara Loe, Becky Allen, Ben LeCompte, Benjamin Britton, Betsy Savercool, Betty Sue Flowers, Beverly Sheffield, Bill Bunch, Bill Oliver, Bob Eckardt (Congressman), Brad Hoge, Brigid Shea, Butch Lawson, Cameron Cook, Carl Pickhart, Carolyn Remesat, Catfish Kelley, Cherokee Dalehite, Dan Inman, Dan Morris, Daniel Llanes, Daryl Andrews, David Holland, David Jewell, David Lauterstein, Debbie Gardiner, Deborah Corry, Dick Drobnick, Dixie Beal, Dorothy Richter, Dr. Joe Maneul Martin, Duke Villarini, Ed Groszewski, Eddie Wilson, Eliza Martin, Ellen Geismar, Ellis Williams, Eric Beggs, Eric Ingamells, Francisco Barrientos, Frank Barrientos, Frank Cooksey, Gary Nored, Genevieve Vaughan, Georgeane Burnett, George Coffer, George Seagert, Gerd Bjørhovde, Gioconda (Jo) Bellonci, Ginny Rohlich, Glee Ingram, Glynn Allen, Grady Hillman, Gus Gonzales, Halima Foster, Heather Kennedy, Helen Bryant, Helga Williams, Ingrid Gabríel, Irene Pickhart,

Isabel Gabríel, Ivy Williams, Jim Allen, Jimmy Turner, Joanne Davida, Joe Bruno, Joe Fagen, Joe Halton, John Aielli, John (Jay) Andrews, Jon Beall, John Corry, John Flowers, John Hise, John West, Kam Magor, Karen Varty, Kaya Pinchback, Kevin Corry, Kip Holm, Konstantin Kuzminsky, Larry Davida, Lael Seagert, Leigh VanKirk, Laure Hoffman, Lauren Jabon, Lelia Eastburn, Liz Andrews, Lois Sheffield, Lori McClure, Jane Pitkin, Marasri Eurich, Margie Allen, Mark Gentle, Mark Hellman, Maria Wells, Marion Holbrook, Marshall Frech, Mary Rohlich, Marilyn Prengler, Marilyn Reeder, Matt Schickle, Megan Bright, Michael Polacheck, Michelle Lilliker, Molly Bean, Molly Britton, Nathan Coburn, Nick Crews, Pam Knight, Pat Otis, Patsy Jimenez, Peach Reynolds, Pete Connely, Peter Bellonci, Priscilla Lightsey, Reggie Grue, Rick Wright, Robert Corbin, Robert (Cliff) Hammond, Robin Britton, Robin Cravey, Ron Boatright Jr, Ron Davis, Rosa Davida, Sally Jacques, Sarah Bolz, Sarah Searight, Saundra (Vicky) Kirk, Scott Cook, Scott Greer, Scott Lackey, Sghot MacKenzie, Shudde Fath, Sigurd Severson, Stephen Wolleben, Steve Frost, Steve Sawhill, Susan Lee Solar, Tibb Burnett, Tina Marsh, Tom Blesch, William E. Bright.

Swimming in Hope

The sun rolled out like waves of platinum across the water from the Mediterranean Sea, the Indian Ocean, from continent to island to ocean to desert. From valley to temple, the sun rolled. It rolled and was greeted by revelers, dancers in veils, old men chanting into the wind, people kissing, children laughing, and everywhere it rose to waves and waves of almost universal optimism. The people of the earth turned their best faces to the new millennium, like plants turn to light, like old people gleam into eternity. I took a close-up photograph of John West's polar bear warm-ups. Swimmers gathered. I began collecting stories from old timers, from polar bears who swim all winter. I'm one. Jane said I should write about swimming with arthritis. It is the only time she doesn't hurt. Dorothy and I were trying to remember the first time we swam in Barton Springs and couldn't. Lots of swimmers can't. Barbara remembers that it saved her life. Dan's back in the water after a bout of pneumonia. He quotes Beverly who said swimming was one of his three favorite things to do in a horizontal position, talks about his *elevens*. I've watched Dan do eleven strokes between breaths. He works up to it, first *fives*, then *sevens*, then *nines* and finally *elevens*. He says when he started swimming, before it became automatic, it was an effort to get to the pool. Now it is an effort not to. The automatic part is what's important. When a child learns to read, each letter, then each word is a struggle. Then it's automatic, like a heart beat, like breath. By the time Dan hits the *elevens* he's completely focused, energy so precisely spent if he raises his head to look up, he feels it in the pit of his stomach. It's like flying. It's freedom. He says when he was a child he used to drink from the hose in the side yard, trying to see how long he could go without breathing. He thought if he were drinking water he wouldn't have to breathe. We swim into a kind of being that is so completely physical the person and the medium are seamless — like sex, like Zen, like omnipresence. Winter swimmers don't do it for the discipline. We do it to transcend. It is a fabulous high, like the wave of optimism that rolled around the planet declaring today, today, today and again today. Now. This is it. And the people who gather here are also it, a community on the edge of a millennium, seamlessly threading time. Pat Otis says when she swims she watches the edge lines disappear between her skin and the water until she feels that every cell of her is water and every part of the water is part of her, no edges, a blue planet rolling around a fire ball in space, a quickening of hope around the world.

Swimming to Greenwich

My intent was to be swimming when Greenwich Time
switched from 1999 to 2000, but I was late
which Eric pointed out as I arrived listening
to Gary laugh. Gary has the best laugh anywhere.

Air temperature drifted to the forties.
The water was teal blue and silver. Globs
of light skittered across arcs of rippling black, cold night.

I kicked into back dolphins above the spring where
light spun like dust as I dove upside down back to winter
and the night, no thoughts, an exquisite green chill.

Beverly's spiral Christmas tree moved alongside me against
a skyline spotted with sequined light. The car heater
blasted delicious, red hot air that beckoned sleep.

My life is cracked in half as time rolls from millennium
to millennium. I, who am always ravenous, will barely taste
the new one, cannot read its pulse. Time spills like creek
water through a ten-sided sieve, is grainy and relentless.

When time rolled over in Austin, we were at home.
The neighborhood filled up with shouts, fire crackers,
the clatter of 256,000 people ten blocks away.

The peace and beauty that are possible,
I find in our magnificent emerald water which
is a glyph of the universe, and in love that surges
all around us — with its orchestra of chaos.

Bonding to the Creek

I can't remember the first time I swam in Barton Springs, though I recall relearning how to breathe in cold water. Carl asked me when I bonded to the creek which flashed me back to the mountains in Pennsylvania. I may have bonded to the water here before I saw Barton Springs — a scent in the air of fresh water, mist. I swam every day, but didn't consider myself a lapper or even a year around swimmer until a December after-noon in the mid-eighties, when Jimmy Turner, in sign language, said, *You are too much in commerce who belongs to the water of the universe.* When I got to the pool, Pete was balancing his body on one hand like an Olympic gymnast, said winter swimming was the most exquisite experience possible. I knew about the warm bubble around the water on a sunny day, knew to lie out on rocks full of solar heat. Ron Boatright Jr. said his family camped beside pool. He could hear his parents call the children to breakfast when they were swimming in the shallow end. Irene was afraid to do the crawl for more than fifty years until it occurred to her she could exhale into the water when she turned her face down, inhale as she turned out. She used to breathe both ways on the side turn, which made her choke. At first it was terrifying. Now she can swim free style. She is looking for opportunities to change more habits that don't work. Dixie Beal had a recurring childhood dream about a green pool that filled him with joy. When he discovered Barton Springs, it was exactly the water that he dreamed. Later he learned his parents had brought him here, once, when he was an infant. Some babies bond to skin, some to soft cotton sheets. I bonded to the water. Jo says what draws us to babies is the same thing that bonds us to the spring — a deep essential connection to the beginning of life.

Photo by Marasri Eurich

Cormorant

Today
I watched a Cormorant
slide to a landing,
float, dive,
swim under me,
catch something,
swim back up,
float into
a paddle, collapse into
a goofy
running start,
and fly.

Swimming in Apples

> *"If you expand the size of an apple to the size of the world, then the atoms in the apple would be the size of the apple you started with."*
> Richard Feynman, Los Alamos Project,
> an inventor of the atomic bomb.

When Francisco's baby teeth were firm enough to bite into an apple, bite marks snaked around the surface of *red* like a trail. Jump scale. Imagine a red earth, with leaves and a stem, seeds spewing out of a volcano instead of molten stone. Jump scale again. Imagine small apple atoms jigging around inside an earth-sized apple, ready to be sliced, split, soft juice dripping off the chin of a giant. I can't get through a day without falling into a blood sugar hole in the afternoon, which will disappear if I eat an apple. Yesterday Francisco reminded me to go to the grocery store to get snacks for my swimming bag. I drew an X on my knuckle so I would remember, *power bars, granola bars, fruit.* Karen brings apples for the children, and tangelos. We read a children's story about Johnny Apple-seed who traveled everywhere planting trees, which appeals to me more than the story of a naked woman whose hunger for a piece of fruit, or for
a man, condemned us to centuries of mayhem. Scott told me he *prefers knowledge to the rustic imbecility of the founding couple.* I would have known Adam. What I like about apples is the way they taste. And they cheer me up. If I want knowledge I'll screw something up and then try to fix it. Or read a book. Apples don't make me smart — except the one Feynman scaled up to the size of the earth. That one makes my mind work better than it used to, when nature made sense and no one thought to blow up atoms. When I was a child apples made me hungry. Can we assume this raw hunger of mine is related to Feynman's apple which grew so vast? What is ethics to someone capable of inventing an atomic bomb in war time? On Halloween, children in the American Midwest bob for apples. The trick is (while blindfolded, hands tied behind your back) to catch hold of an apple in a bucket of very cold water—catch hold of it with your teeth, before you run out of breath. If you can do that, you win something, or you get to eat the apple. I'll always do that, if I get the apple. I'll eat it. Even if it is a very, very, very large apple — no hands necessary, just ravenous curiosity. But I'd stop short of the explosion, at least I hope I would.

Twilight

Night
comes to us
over green water
released from a dam.

Cold, deep
water flows emerald
beneath the belly
of a Mallard duck.

Wind stills,
for an instant,
roughs up again.

Cold, velvet wind
pushes
slate clear
water to a ripple.

To hold back
the night,
we press
our mouths
against a song.

Crows, Blackbirds, Black Suits

Emerald cold water, still as I enter, parts for the swimmer I am in a dream and this morning, in fact. *Onetwothree — breathe. Onetwothree — breathe*, as I turn on the fourth stroke, I can see it, emerald water, leveling white caps, air bubbles. Beyond that are crows, vultures, black suits. My arms lap, legs scissor, breath percolates, hands cup; water drops arc, eyes shift every fourth stroke, from subterranean vision, to fast shafts of seeing that race across air. And the river moves gently, cold emerald spirals rise up from the center of the springs I swim over. They pulse like a heartbeat, heart of earth, water, emerald cold water, emerald essence of water, swirling with the turn of the planet, mercurial underneath thunder sky. I blend with the river, exhaling, inhaling, listening to the slow sound of breath under water. There's no hurry, once I'm moving, cold is a part of me, hair snaps my face, wet, like snakes or a rope. I am one with the cold, its cool emerald essence. *Onetwothree — breathe, Onetwothree — breathe.* Black birds or hawks, vultures it looks like, men in black suits, silhouettes against thunder sky, ominous against thunder sky, one woman, swimming alone in the water. Above me, engineers are talking to television. *We can tear up the aquifer and not hurt it, pie charts and graphs prove it.* They are men in black suits, their beards are diplomas with no courses in literature or ethics, philosophy or art. They are standing on a hill above the cold water, making pronouncements, backs turned to the water, words pouring out. Minds light on experience, brood with theory. I call out, *Come, stand in the water. At least turn and look at it!* Cameras click, microphones are netted against wind, thundersky rumbles disgust. *Onetwothree — breathe, onetwothree — breathe*, crow feet, beak arms, thunder mouthed babbling, death to the planet. A warning. A warning.

Finding Becky

My son tells
me if I see
Becky —
Tell
her to come
see me.

I find
only the shape
of her face
in the
man
who is her
father.

Maybe
next time.

Lappers

My first lap is slow unless I'm cold or angry, in which case, it's full of growls bubbling into dark green depths, arms slapping water, hard kicks that move me too fast, pull a muscle in my shoulder. My first lap is stiff. I can't catch my breath. Eric's first lap surges full of power that bursts out, strong kicking, long arms cutting into the water. His last lap is slow. Barbara and Cherokee swim in a kind of unison which is gentle and rhythmic. The only time you can see Karen in the water is when she is pregnant, otherwise she dematerializes. Frank looks where he's going and rolls to miss me when I plow into him. It takes me forever to do a mile, and sometimes I get cold, or bored. My fourth lap is fast. Karen says it is because I want to get out. Debbie swims on her back, gently oblivious to all of us, and we have learned to mostly dodge her. Joe swims underwater collecting things people drop. Ben swam laps for twenty-four hours straight before he swam across the Atlantic, a two person sailboat alongside, magnetic field to keep predators away. Dan can do fifteen strokes before he has to breathe. One Steve tries to swim across the pool and back under water. One Marilyn kicks and splashes in delightful syncopated jerks and surges, bell clear voice calling to everyone along both sides of the pool. She is the Victor Borge of the breast stroke. One day Barbara told Jo she was going to swim circles around Marilyn, and then did it. Armin watches (adoringly) Carolyn swim, or swims alongside her. The other Steve motors back and forth, disappearing like Karen into the substance of the pool, and re-emerges an hour later smiling like the happy otter tattoo on his arm. George water jogs wearing a straw hat from Mexico. Leal swims perfectly then stretches on the hill. John Aielli and I once swam to the dam, leaned our heads backwards off the edge and watched the sun set upside down. Daryl and Becky race across the deepest part of the pool from the old Pecan tree to the diving board. One wins. The other claims to have won. Matt's stroke is lifeguard perfect except he only breathes on one side. Sghot, the lifeguard who is a painter, cut off his rainbow colored dreads when he returned to Michigan, and shaved. I'm trying to remember if I ever saw him in the water. I've never seen Duke in the water, though someone said a photograph exists. Dr. Joe and Lori named their children after our springs. They swim perfectly. One morning Butch said, *You're in my lane*. I said, *What's a lane?* and he said, *Anything you want it to be*. I used to end my noon hour lap at the same time a tall and charming swimmer (who was our mayor) began his swim. Now I swim with Congressman

Continued

Eckardt, one of the architects of Texas liberal politics. Robert comes several times a day and is much more complicated than he appears to be. He moves quickly to keep from sinking like a stone. The other Marilyn says the healing power of our water keeps her alive. Catfish swims for pleasure at the most beautiful time of day, is a magnet for the golden light. Jim dives in, gets right back out. Ellen spends as much time as possible at the pool. Patsy side strokes and chats with friends down to the dam and back at night. John Flowers says swimming makes his mind settle to the peaceful bottom like a smooth stone resting in eternity. Molly, an attorney and environmental activist, swims a half mile at the warmest time of day all year around. She says it gives her peace.

I Turn into a Fish

Quicksilver disks of air
emulsify the human shape
so all that's left
are long wet eyelashes
crow feet eyes,
translucent gold.

The belly parts
green moss along the bottom
of the creek.

I suck in algae
blow out silver balls
of air.

The head elongates,
mouth puckers
to an 0.

I turn into a fish.
One yellow fin,
undulates
through cold thick time
and there is hunger
on the fish brain.

I am a swift,
small wedge of life,
loose
between
a rose smudged dawn
and
the enchantment
of blue.

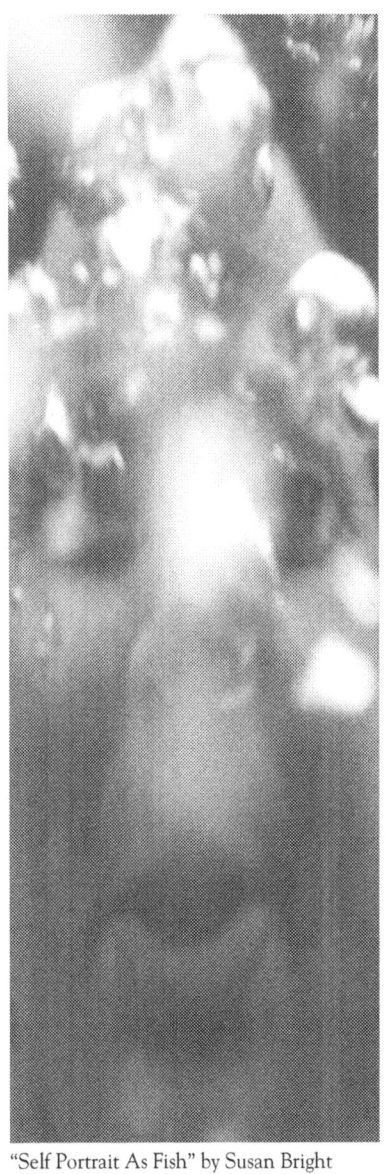

"Self Portrait As Fish" by Susan Bright

Soup

Eventually the water was bound to turn up someone who accomplished the ocean swim to Catalina Island I was invited to attempt, after an over zealous bibliographer listed *Swimming the English Channel* in *Triathlon* magazine. I declined, saying I was a poet, a pleasure swimmer, that an ocean swim to Catalina Island would kill me. Eric said I should have gone. I said, *Are you kidding?* and he said, *You could do it*, which surprised me because I still think it would kill me. Today I told the story to someone who has done it. Stephen, one of our winter guards, said twenty people swam eight or nine miles on a warm, calm day. Kayakers paddled along and a life boat was always in sight. He said much of the distance was vertical. He was exhausted and not sure he could make landfall. Ocean swimmers do what other swimmers do, but under duress. Stephen said sharks off the Southern California coast shy away from people but up north they don't, said his brother-in-law was surfing off Point Reyes in North San Francisco on a clear water day, holding onto a surf board, waiting for a wave, when he saw something with a gray hammer face the size of a car coming at him from the depths. I'm happy on the beach at Point Reyes. Surfers walk down to waves that swell above their heads when they stand on shore, and the water is in the low fifties. Jay says scientists who study sharks, attract them off Point Reyes by floating surf boards around the observation platform. I've seen Catalina Island from the air — large estates, wide beaches. I wonder if I could swim eight ocean miles, or any. It would take six hours on a calm day. He said they angle in from the south. If they swam straight at the island, sea currents would pull them quickly in, which sounds sensible to me. Stephen said he didn't mind the idea of a shark attack, *You'd go quickly*. I don't care to be eaten by a fish. He admitted that his brother-in-law floated carefully to a boulder and then walked ashore at low tide the day he saw a shark the size of a car. *You're basically food in there*, Stephen said. *It's a huge soup pot.*

Catch of the Day

I am learning
not to want
fish that elude
the plate
or try to chart
the currents of their
drift.

Instead
I take the catch
of the day.
Its warm flesh
inside me
is luxurious enough—
abates my hunger nicely.

My own
swimming life suits
the moment—
I cut through water
at my own pace
in perfect cadence.
This is real.
I trust it.

Things That Weren't Lost

Patsy lost Susan Lee Solar's earth mother goddess Gaia in the water and Michael found it the next night, a flash of gold, like the small suns that dance on water which flows deep teal blue to black at night. Helga said *a woman* (we often don't know people's names although we see them every day and greet each other on the street with lines like, *I didn't recognize you with your clothes on*, or *You don't look bad in clothes*) lost a two thousand dollar diamond ring in the deep part of the pool above the springs. It turned up later at the desk. Helga lost her bridge one time and found that too. My son comments on major shrinkage when he jumps in the pool, but that also returns. Tibb wondered if someone hadn't lost their virginity in our water, but I think it might be too cold. Scott told me he came upon a couple making love in one of the guard chairs. They were elevated, up high on a platform, for increased visibility. Perhaps the notion came on the couple quickly, or possibly they didn't think anyone would notice. I'm convinced people make love alongside the pool all the time, though I've never done it. Joe has a treasure trove of things he's found at the bottom of the pool. One Sunday afternoon he showed me rings and necklaces, barrettes, crosses, earrings, money — ones, tens, coins and a few twenties. I wanted to make a list but he said not to, that he wanted to retire on his treasure trove, but my guess is the state retirement system will have a higher yield. Actually the valuable things he's found diving, he's given back, a Rolex watch, for instance. Yesterday I lost a pair of blue hand paddles which I bought the day before. Karen lost the kick board she loaned, then gave to me last summer. I'm not convinced one can lose anything important in this water, except the water itself. We could lose that. If we're not careful.

Riding the Currents

I want to ride the currents,
find light in the shallows
of the emerald water,
cool under an August sun
that heats Texas to a sizzle.

I want to ride the currents,
move my legs back and forth,
kick exactly these red flippers
that push me through
the water, four long laps
in cold emerald light—
an elegant, rich mile.

I want to sit alongside
Barton Springs and talk
to my friends, the swimmers
who have been meeting here
for years, new swimmers,
water people whose eyes are
clear as emerald, and true.

I want to ride the currents,
draft the swimming god,
smooth the jagged edges
of me that shred any hope
of serenity. I want to disappear
into the water, no seams.

I want to ride the currents,
not always fight them,
kick back and stretch,
swim further today
than I could yesterday,
and faster because it makes
me strong, because
it calms me down.

Cat Napping at the Pool

Cats make good fajitas, I hear Eric say. Michelle says he should have used the cat to paint his house, which judging from the paint on his arm, he'd been trying to accomplish. But he said, *I am painting my arm. I'm not finished yet*, and went on to say he was also painting the top of his van, the driveway and a tarp he dragged around from room to room which got me going about the time I painted our wooden house on Dexter Street with white paint and blue trim, in July. It was 107 by noon. I had to scrape before I could paint. It kept me occupied for weeks. A vision has stayed with me for years. Jay is walking alongside the house. I am on a ladder scraping paint with a three inch scraper. In the back pocket of his jeans is a paint scraper eight inches wide. Eric is saying he didn't know cats could make *fajitas* — cut up onions, scoop out sour cream, cut cilantro, lime, grate cheese. Michelle says she can't get her cats to do anything. Mine are useless too. One chases the cat across the street, across the street. The Calico who lives in my bedroom, snuggles on my chest every time I lie down, and then digs her claws into my throat. I've forgotten for a moment the hollow ache that's settled into my chest. I've had a cat nap, slip into the water, do a mile with the kickboard Karen gave me and long flippers, keeping my head from getting wet in deference to the doctor who no longer tells me to stay out of the water when I get swimmer's ear. Yesterday, she ran what sounded like a fire hose through both ears to get out wax and gave me medicine that works fast. The water is full of algae. Kip is swimming side stroke to the dam. Steven is drinking coffee and eating a slice of homemade banana bread on guard stand one. I've stopped thinking, at least when I get out I can't call back anything important. I was trying to kick harder. I was trying to steer around the larger algae globs. I was trying to get out from under the anguish pressing against my soul. I'm worried that I'll get used to it, forget to laugh, forget the people in my life who are miracles, focus on pain instead of the emerald surge of life around me.

The Swimming Angel

Water wings, the purest light you can imagine, sky blue eyes like mother,
a nudge, soft feathers, lifting —

Something like a low haze, crystal rain-spikes soft on skin
as water falls from the tourmaline ceramic bowl of sky —

Loops of night on limestone under water, etchings more delicate
than a shudder, bonding with the unknowable.

Love comes when I can open my soul, slow down the chaos,
stand with it, a low fog, luminescent, new —

The dew point, an applique gown made in the Philippines, ice crust on
melt, crisp art paper, white corn flower, strange

alphabets, clear sand, ginger layers of dust, salt and thirst,
desire —

An exactly white presence, hovering where my elbow pops
out of water between draughts of air —

A being so true it makes me laugh to think of the hours she
graced my life —

before I felt the velvet tip of her invisible breast —

Swimming Back to Our Senses

I dive into the sensual joy of it, August light hot on me like a lover.
I am alive, move my arms out from center, frog kick, roll over on my back, windmill into a flurry of children. Yesterday Barbara and Cherokee brought Willow to the pool for the first time. She's three weeks old, cried when Barbara gave her a breast cold from the water. Amiten, whom I've known since he was a child, is guarding near the dam. He raises two fingers as I swim past. Frank and Karen leap into the water. The pool is full of algae. Crowds are filling up skin hill. When my son was small, we wound our way through the bathers once, past a woman sunbathing topless. Everyone was looking at her, pretending not to, or blatantly looking, so the man whose face my son stepped on didn't see him coming. This year lots of women and some men are wearing g-string bikinis. The air is hot and visceral. Bathers suck lemons and drink bottled water. Young children play running games at the top of the hill, past teenagers with their world slightly askew. It is 114 degrees and the temperature hasn't dropped below three digits in six weeks. Earth is hot and cracked. People all over town are soak-watering trees. I have been swimming with my head out of the water, which is bleaching my hair and making my skin dark. It is slow going, an exercise in patience, gives me time to watch the explosion of sensuality that is this place — naked babies, every kind of body, skin color, shape, personality and the lack of it. The raft people, slick with sun oil, pile up at the dam. Five to seven thousand people will come here today, lie out in the sun then cool off in the water. They'll sit under the trees, talk to each other, look and not touch, or touch and not look at all of us swimming, however we can, back to our senses.

Egg

At first it was a game. Our son would cover himself with pillows and pretend to be an egg. We'd root around, open drawers, *No, not in the drawer. Look under the bed. I thought I heard . . . It's awfully dusty, don't you think?* We'd check to see if he'd been flushed down the commode, pretend not to hear him giggle. When the time seemed right, we'd find the egg, *Maybe it's going to hatch. What do you think it will be? I have no idea, what do you think?* *Well,* we'd hear more giggles, or car engine sounds, sometimes barking, or small meowing, sometimes a perfect infant brawl, *Maybe it's a motorcycle?* We'd guess until we came upon the thing he wanted to be. He liked to hatch into a truck, a kitty. He liked to be a baby too, would crawl around, make perfect baby sounds so you knew he had, in fact, become his infant self. Later there were other eggs beginning with an obsidian one I got him the day his twin brother appeared. After that I got him an egg every Easter and for his birthday — soap stone eggs, onyx from Mexico, an azurite egg from Tucson, one made out of Picasso Stone, a malachite egg with a flower and a small opera theater in its green design. Once I found a *milagro* egg from Mexico, tin with miracles scattered about — a star, a cat, Guadalupe, somebody's leg, an arm, a heart, visceral like a real one, a bear, a cow, a chicken, somebody's house, the moon, someone praying, the sun, a stalk of corn, someone's parents. We brought him an amber egg the year we weren't sure he'd live another week, a rose quartz one the year we weren't sure how we'd endure another minute. And he kept hatching, broke out of every mold, covered himself with tattoos more complex than the *milagro* egg. One egg from Bali was carved out of wood, nested in a bowl that was itself a chicken. Another was an egg man with feet that hang over a shelf. One was fossil stone from Africa. One was a drawing he created of an egg shape ribbon winding around a man holding a staff, walking through stars. I find eggs stashed all over the house. Each one is a phase of this child-now-man's ongoing rebirth. As my own flow of eggs grows sluggish, there's a shell to me that's cracking. Something wet and slick is swimming out to air — the woman that small child birthed, all that I am and never was until a small adopted boy showed up, invented a game that we called *egg*.

Riddle of the River

I am at a gathering of generations.
There has been a disturbance
having to do with children
after which the old people
draw lots.
I want to play but it's not
my turn.

Next to the river
a small person with a gleaming face,
a fairy or a druid,
is telling me how to live with
children. *You love them.*
she says.

My mother is growing smaller
and smaller —
smaller.
I reach down to pick her up.
She protests.
*If you carry me I'll never
walk again,*
but she is now
an infant
and I hold her in my arms.

We begin a journey.
I am walking through mountains.
My eyes distort the scale of
place as we climb and thread
around ravines and crevices.

Suddenly there are no options —
except a thousand foot drop
down to the desert,
jagged rocks,

red, earthen in color,
above jutting peaks,
no vegetation,
sharpness pointing at the sky.

I am holding
the infant that is my mother
when I notice it might be possible
to take another turn,
which I do
and step nicely down
to a quaint village
inhabited by people and vegetation,
even a river.

It is cold.
I meet a tall man who walks
alongside me
as if he belonged.
I ask him if he needs his coat.
There is one in his back pack.
He gives it to me
grudgingly,
saying I should have
one of my own.
I don't.
I tell him the baby is cold,
who is my mother,
and if he will carry her
he can have the coat.

The man is brilliant
and takes long steps,
my father in his youth.
I am my young mother before
I was born.
Who is the babe
in arms?

Swimming in Socks

I live with people who produce baskets and more baskets of white laundered and bleached socks. No one folds or sorts. When one needs socks, he appears alongside the bed and lines them side by side like long fish until a mate turns up. If the spirit moves him, he bundles the rest of the whites back into a basket. This morning three people sorted whites and none was moved to clear away what turned into a bed full of mismatched socks. I'd been dreaming of water, dove into a lake that thickened to styrofoam, chlorinated mesh, thick chemical water with feathers in it. It was a strange swimming dream from which I awoke surrounded by socks. Jo wears socks when she swims to keep her long red flippers from blistering her feet. One summer she figured out ways to spend most of her time at the pool. In the mornings she took care of Francisco. All the swimmers fell in love with him. Jo said, *This is the best*, meaning the water, sunlight, the people, Francisco paddling and gurgling. I sat alongside the water and fed him the first day he ate with a spoon. Lately he's older. We read stories about trucks or bears while Karen, his mother, swims. A community of mothers and fathers and babies gathers alongside the pool — Francisco and his parents, Karen and Frank and baby Esmeralda; Deborah, John, young Kevin and Matthew; Lori, Joe and their children, Eliza and Julia Parthenia; Lauren, Peter, the twins and Lucy; Scott, Priscilla and Cameron; Ingrid and Isabel. Parents take turns watching the children. My sons grew up here. Our street was full of urban occurrences that cause parents to lose sleep. At the pool I could let them play freely. Daryl, Becky, Margie, Anna, Halima, and sometimes Nick used to pound limestone on the sidewalk to make *milk* or gather globs of green algae to throw at each other. They found frogs in the limestone ledge, held them carefully in their small hands, then placed them back in small frog caves. There are alien encounter myths in the local frog song, and a giant story. You can hear it in the change of pitch. When the boys were small it was easy to tell their socks from Jay's. Now they all wear the same socks. I find them everywhere. The dogs take them out in the yard to play tug. Jay uses them to wax the car. When one of them finds two socks that match he says *Yes!*

Getting Organized

I have been trying to get organized, but what feels true to me is that everything is swirling all the time and I lose focus, sail into some reverie, then crash back to a riot of paper, personality, deadlines which somehow I meet while holding everything I want at bay. I have time for listening to the water but none to answer my phone when I get back to work. Yesterday I swam a mile and then, endorphins dancing, watched clouds drift through swirls of pecan leaves, nut cases about to drop, dropping too soon, still encased in green, small miracles that burst out of a tree so twisted and off balance it's held up by two steel poles, which I lean against to stretch. I fed grackles and park pigeons the crumbled up pieces of two power bars. A pigeon hopped onto my lap. One of the baby grackles was cross-billed, had to slide its head sideways on the concrete walk to pick up crumbs I threw off to the side, shooing the other birds away. I needn't have been so protective. The broken one was fierce. Park pigeons roost on the roof of the bird-woman's trailer, swoop about the park in a flock of subtle color. They eat out of our hands because she has hand fed chicks for years. Duke sets peanuts on the office windowsill. Grackles will take them from his hand, squirrels will take them from his mouth. Scott says one got so fat it fell out of a tree. There are single-cell amoebae who live alone and simply, unless conditions stress them, no water, for example, in the face of which they band together and begin to swirl in a matrix that looks like a spiral galaxy if you see it in three dimensions. Then, some of these single cell beings, *Dictyostelia* is their name, turn into something like an elevator, while the rest of them keep being a spiral of amoebae, which gets pushed up by the changelings so wind can blow the colony someplace wet. They have this way of organizing that looks like chaos and is so minuscule we can't see it occur, don't recognize their fierce order, or mourn the ones left behind to die. Pecan leaves are spiral clusters of small green sliver moons. If you stare at them long enough you can see it. If you let the emerald water disorient you, if you know how to drift across realities that jump scale, things fall in place. It's possible to focus, get some work done, and still know the urge to fly off, the drift of migration, the sacrifice.

Diving off the Hancock Center

I take deep steps
in Chicago
sinking into
saturate
black earth,
all the blues
of the lake,
wind,
the child I was,
my parent's grief,
an American dream
that never stopped
breaking,
the best
of now.

Let's go up.
he gestures.
I remember the
elevator
as my ears pop.
And the view —
shocking,
magnificent.

I wonder
how long it will
take him to run out
of architecture
to identify,
this man
who keeps knowing
and knowing,
who I
dumbfound.
Then I dive.

I dive fast,
deeper than blue,
though glitter,
through Chicago jazz
in a taxicab
on Lake Shore Drive.
I stop holding on.
I'm not falling.
It's a dive,
one hell of a dive.

Life is a horizontal fall.
      (Jean Cocteau)

— is something like
this long dive
that is essential,
that I carry
close
as the air
I dive into,
or the water
I dive through,
pushing off
from
blue —

Save

I was talking to Steve when we saw somebody streak from the grassy area above the diving board, jump the ledge, swim across the pool and pull someone out. None of the guards saw it until Nate (who was manager last year) had the save, a classic — pull one wrist, turn the victim in the water, hook your arm over their shoulder, scissor kick out. I wanted to know why Nate, who wasn't working, got there before four guards on duty, and he said it was experience. It's also chance. I've never been a guard but I pulled someone out. Frank, who was a guard for years, beat everyone in a few months ago. Cliff had the misfortune of being the one to find a drowned man suspended two feet under water several years ago. Which is not to say our guards aren't paying attention, but the pool has always been understaffed. It's hard to understand why, since it makes a huge amount of money. Today the save was Nate's. He was no sooner back under the trees talking to Sara when she said, *There's a guy on the other side of the fence trying to get in.* I didn't see anyone, but Nate did. About the time she caught on, Nate was at the fence running him off and Sara was saying, *He's not trying to get in, he's trying to get off.* Other than that it was a peaceful day at the pool. Robin, who has two teenagers, was subdued. Francisco has the flu and didn't come so I had no one to read stories to. Steve is going to paint his kitchen, and I am going to finish a book I've been working on for years. A water line across the street spewed water to the treetops. There's a hurricane about to make landfall on the Texas coast. One of my swimming dogs once pulled a woman out of Barton Creek. She couldn't swim, slipped off a ledge, was floundering. Before anyone noticed, Spud, a Shepherd/Ridgeback mix, closed his massive jaws around her arm and pulled her back to shore. He received enormous praise for this. So much he plunged back in to pull out the next person who swam past, and the next. I'm like that, better at trying for a save than knowing when to stop.

Swimming in the Shallows

There is shallow beauty —
light reflecting from stones in
ripples as wind touches the surface.

There are perhaps threads of being
that transcend time.
If I jump scale, I get lost, fast.

Today I opt for the shallows.
I am able to sweep.
I am able to do laundry and cook.

I am able to clear off my desk.
I am unable to do anything
complex.

I can't look at the cold truth
of anything
for long.

What I am able to do
is ride the shallows. Anything
else is inconceivable.

I can float.
That's about it.
Maybe take a nap.

Unraveling

I am on Norwegian television when a vest I'm wearing begins to unravel. Between poems and questions, I pull out a handful of embroidery thread. There is no way to cut, so I tuck the stuff under my belt. I step out of Barton Springs after a mile swim, wrap a towel which is unraveling around my waist. I pull a long red thread, tell Annette I have been playing chess with Descartes. Steve says, *Descartes was good at chess*. I am stretching the cramps out of my calf muscles. I read in the *Financial Times* that understanding Russia is like playing three dimensional chess in a fluid state. There is a strain of pigs that produces universal organs that can be transplanted, with a few problems, into human beings, the problems being: 1. the recipient might get a pig version of AIDS and 2. Pig cells remain in the blood indefinitely so although one may live longer one is, at least partially, a pig. I blur my eyes to enhance the rivers between letters on the page. I know Descartes as well as anyone. The fabric of what's given is unraveling. When he notices it, he will assume another fabric which will again unravel. He will fix it quickly and well. I can't play chess with him, better to crack a joke. It is possible to swim down to the center of the spring, place your hands over its pulse. As you rise, blue light filters through emerald water and your lungs want to burst. I've been too smart, brilliantly stupid, too fast, too old, absolutely uncertain, and I've been perfect. I've let everything unravel and I've found myself threaded to a stubborn kind of genius that disappears and springs back. The other day I was cuffed in the neck by a faith healer who was swimming backwards. His white hair, when it dries, threads in ringlets half way down his back. The fact is anything we do or know can be unraveled. Find a thread, and pull. Anything can come apart. The trick is to hold something together — love or truth or passion, red or raw sienna or grace — long enough to say its name, before it comes undone.

Coming Up For Air

I dove so swiftly
into the past
I nearly drowned,
a girl growing up,
a girl who was an artist,
whose brother died
which made me
a mirror of death —
which I knew to refute.

I knew this
when I dove into
toxic water
next
to a mountain
of asbestos,
next
to a tannery,
next
to a jet fuel dump.

Now
I am swimming
to light,
out of suffocating
grief, and its
cruel siblings.

The round bubbles
of my soul
are flat pewter disks
that flutter
as I come
up for air.

Perspective

It's like this, Eric said to one of the guards. He was talking about ocean guarding, was pointing at the far side of the pool where children were splashing in bright emerald water. The spring was swirling up. The hill was rising above pecan trees and cedars, pin oaks and elm trees, past the soccer fields, past the top of the hill where I live, past the lower hill where our rent house is being painted gray with dark green windows, past the school we helped found, past the city where high tech, hot air, light and traffic arrange themselves in a thick urban sprawl, past the interstate highway system which holds him in a matrix of work and personality, past the people in his life, past boundaries between states. Eric was seeing east to the Atlantic coast, was standing in a sea wind, tasting salt water, feeling the tight way it stays your skin. He was standing on the beach in the Florida Keys where he worked as a life guard, which explains his way of swimming. He was standing alongside a spring in a city completely landlocked. I was looking across the pool at a bunch of children one of whom had just tried to walk off with my red flippers, the ones Karen gave me last summer, after Jo gave them to her before she moved to Italy for a year of Montessori training, after she used them for five years and then went on to wider ones, with more thrust, the red flippers my new dog with one brown and one blue eye just ate. Ingrid told me they originally belonged to Steve, who said he *sort of remembered having a red pair of flippers,* but his were wide, mine have been trimmed. We think Jo did it. All of which happened before Eric came to Austin, before his children were born, before he stood alongside the pool, looked across and seeing the Atlantic ocean which cannot be contained, said, *It's just like this,* his long arm gesturing at the arc of the horizon, *except there's nothing out there.*

Swimming in Negation

Sometimes
nothing works
as well
as
anything.

So
I do it.

What the River Knows

In dream Steve comes to the pool, but the water has receded and the gates are closed. The guards ask him if he wants to see the place *where the water is made*. They take him around behind the dam to a dark, cool place that is exquisite. Brad told me every drop of water that exists on earth has been here since the birth of the planet. In dream Karen Kreps is on a bus in New York City when she gets a dreamtime vision, has flowers and offer-ings in her arms, is told to take them to the Ganges River, which she does, winding through the streets of Calcutta, until she sees the river's edge, dives in and begins to swim under water deeper, deeper until she runs out of breath and still she keeps on diving, carrying the flowers with her. Eventually she swims to a large circle of fire where an initiation begins. Scott is swimming in a dreamtime Barton Springs and becomes thirsty, but doesn't have permission to drink the water until a loud voice says, *Go Ahead. Drink.* Water pours, clear and cool, all through him, quenching a vast thirst. It's as if the river is trying to speak to us. The ones who come here find a liquid kind of truth. Eric dreams of breathing under water, at first seems to be suffocating, then remembers he is swimming, takes a deep, full breath — of water. Karen Varty tells me she sometimes gets air before she turns her head to the side, as if she's pulling it directly from the water. Ellen says she has done that too. If I am out of the water more than a week, I dream swim, sometimes in a wide river that's moving fast, is full of boats and other swimmers, full of debris and implements of civilization which don't belong in water, sky scrapers, for example, or airports, an art museum. Becky swims in golden underwater light and breathes its grace which is her own. The meditation I use to shield my loved ones from harm came to me here, alongside the spring, on a winter afternoon, as I stretched out on warm limestone. I think the water is trying to tell us something essential — that it is sentient, for one thing.

Blue Jewel

Guitar riffs scrape the tremor
of my soul when I kick back to rest,
play on the ache where blue jewels
of pain cut pieces of pure soul —
sharp rubies, emeralds, deep blue
sapphires, red so dark it's blue,
blue sound, blue to brass and back,
slivers of an ebony heart ache
I can't swim through,
litany of blue, of blue, blue jewel.

Tonight I swim to emerald cold blue,
want more, count down to blue,
more loneliness, more rain slick oil,
more senseless, thoughtless flight,
another broken door, more rage.
Tonight Chicago jazz and its fine
chunks of diamond brilliant light
are lost, lost, empty, space —
blue jewel, a bray and whine, nothing
to hold on to, no respite,
hollow and wrong, blue jewel.

Tonight I am the deep blue jewel.
Addiction, crazy assholes
who break everything, gentle
ones who leave howling silence
shred me to sand, blue jewel,
like grief, like an eternal wake,
the melody of logic, a shrill mind.
Tonight, a blue lit razor scream —
a lonely deep blue emerald jewel,
cobalt storms, regret, wailing and
relentless blue, blue jewel.

Often I swim in air —

kick back in an airplane seat, look
out at cloud banks, the Sierra
Nevadas, the coast of California, at
Norwegian fjords, slate gray ocean
haze, at Chicago, at the small town
where I grew up, dock yards punching
water like hungry fingers swimming
through Lake Michigan, Lake Huron,
Lake Erie, Lake Superior, Niagara
Falls. I don't tire of flying, crawl and
stretch cupped hands, kick into the
dreamtime, float in the recycled
oxygen the airlines feed us alongside
trays of strange food. We go fast from
place to place, continent to continent,
crossing time zones, kicking off the
edge of yesterday like racers in a
chlorine pool. Sometimes twilight is
an ocean wide. Sometimes I don't reset
my watch. Sometimes I forget to wear
a watch. Once, at the San Francisco
airport, a reporter stuck a microphone
in my face, asked about safety. I was
traveling with a hyper-active boy,
chose bulkhead to get squirming space.
The reporter said I should consider
safety in case of a crash, but there
are no safe seats on an airplane going
down. I dreamed the child and I were
on a plane that dove out of control to
earth. I climbed out the window, slid
down a wing and landed, horrified to
see I'd saved myself and not my son.
Soon he crawled out. I've loved this
child as much as it is possible to love
another person, but he's had to save
himself.

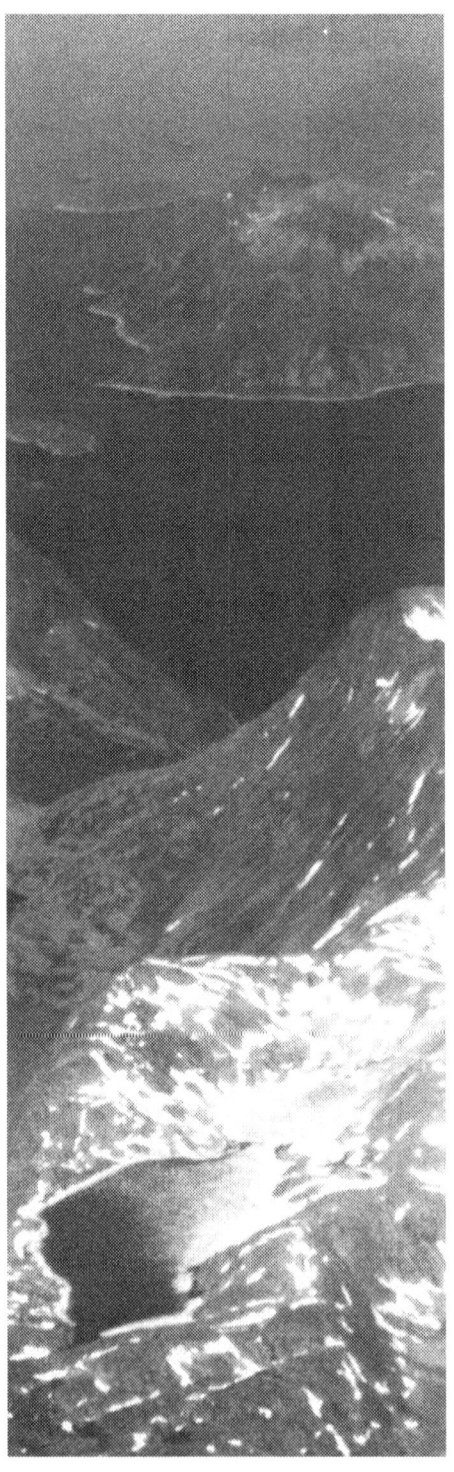

Fijords from the air, by Susan Bright

Inside the Pineapple

from Scott in Barcelona

Because pressure at the foundation is enormous,
the castles are too fast for anyone to live inside, are icons,
a team sport. They teach the ones who climb up forty feet
to fall. They teach the ones below how to receive.

The unlikely fact of it comes from the *colla* (team).
Each person is essential, 120 to a club — more, less. Shirts
announce, for instance, *Fem Pinya*, Catalan for *we make
pineapple*, or maybe *we do pine cone*, or *we bunch*.

What it means comes from the metaphor, something like,
We are solidary, which is apparent as the castle grows in tiers
of people, arms encircled, balanced just so — white jeans,
shirts, bandanas, black belts wound round and around.

Large teams attempt nine tiers, rising in four's, three's, two's —
Bodies pressed together lean to center, perhaps eighty people
at the base. Forty more climb up, stand on each other. It's a sport,
more organized than crowd diving — a balanced soaring knot.

*Never look up. If someone falls on you it's guaranteed to snap
your neck*, is what they tell the foundation weave of people —
a core entanglement, fanned by six close circles, tall to short,
arms stretched up. Interlocking hands become a chair for the legs,

hips, backs of the first tier. Arms push up against the weight.
Festive tunes capable of suspense fly out of horns and pipes.
A single child scrambles to the top of a tower that's alive,
that's not supposed to tear itself apart, but might.

There are different configurations. Small, narrow *castells*
walk about in festival processions. Sometimes a rhythmic
undulation grabs the huge ones. People hold on. Let go.
The child scrambling up and up, freezes, starts down, no time —

Continued

How they rise or fall together is the essence of community.
No injuries, or very few. They rehearse. The body of each
diffuses each impact as they become an acrobatic net of multiple
and wild free falls, forty feet down to the streets of Barcelona.

*A collapsed castell looks like a soup with arms and legs and heads
poking out.* Scott says it happens too fast to hold a mental image
of it. He says the human soup takes five minutes to disperse.
They engineer the take down. They get sport insurance.

Team members support each other, for any reason —
but if you ask someone from another group to plug into a tier,
pick a child up from school, write a reference letter, trade shifts,
cover a mistake, borrow a cell phone or laptop, forget it.

The *We Make Pineapple* team is its own round fruit in a city
jammed between mountains and the sea, a city that inspires perfect
metaphors — Salvadore Dali, Guernica, the towers of Gaudí.
That child on top —

saluting the mayor, who is watching everybody from
the balcony of the *ajuntament* (town hall) — knows who he is,
knows who she is, the taste and feel, the human scent of it,
pungent, sweet.

That Which Connects

When I asked Reggie if he knew the Spirit of the River, he recited measurements, the dynamics of steering a five-story building through a medium in constant flux. Reggie is a riverboat pilot on the Mississippi, caterwauling, exuberant and smart, but he hasn't seen the Spirit of the River. Eric understands water and what spans it, plus he knows the Spirit, says we are incredibly dense on land. Our steps impact a road surface like jack hammers so runners have to go in single file across a bridge but cyclists can wheel across in packs. He says the freeway overpass in Japan that toppled sideways did so because the pillars were too short. Long pillars sway, but short ones can't diffuse the vibration of an earthquake, so they sheer off at the base. The Tacoma Narrows Bridge that tore itself apart in Washington State in the 30s exploded because wind set off a *self-excited vibration*. High winds can turn the Golden Gate Bridge into a wave of pavement hanging in a cloud. The other night I dove out of sleep into a single word that seemed the essential link between large and small. The word was *vibration*. Reality is more like music than geometry. Why shouldn't the universe be a glyph of our essential nature, or vice versa? Mud in a bowl, jiggled to simulate the shuddering release of energy as continental plates drift across each other, rises in oscillations that look like nipples, then sinks to valleys which is how earth turns *liquid* in an earthquake. Eric follows currents to pick up time swimming down stream. My own path through the water is oddly shaped by oncoming traffic, the drift of algae and the tendency I have to pull to the left when I swim upstream, which is a metaphor. Mostly I steer by the tree line, or clouds, and wonder as I go, what connects us to each other, how we flee and how to link back up when we calm down.

Swimming God

For the last three days I have been at the pool
at the same time as the swimming god, a youth,
tall, long legged, large shoulders, a trim build, dark,
sleek, the most sensuous male swimmer I've ever seen.

He doesn't speak to us, but we see him in the water,
a fast swimmer, who stretches with long arms,
powerful shoulders, an easy kick.

He is one of the most attractive men
I've ever seen, an absolute maleness that's not beautiful,
but is completely graceful and magnetic,
making it a joy to be a woman.

I've known several men who actually were
as fabulous as they looked. I can't tell about him,
have just observed him swim, seen him interact

with other swimmers—
primarily by making women blush and blunder.
Today he nodded hello to me. I was shaking water
out of one ear.

I allow myself to appreciate this energy because it means
I am healing from a tight knot of grief.
A man I don't know can fire an erotic response.

I am wide-eyed and alert in his presence.
It means I have come alive.

Winter Swimming

Thin skinned but alive I open my soul to the moment, knowing, for instance, that when I get in the water it will be cold. Swimmers help each other, saying *You can do it*, or *The water is fabulous*, which is true once you get through the barrier. I have learned to embrace cold. Leigh stands on the steps and asks the sun to give her heat. In the winter, on a sunny day, I wear a long green corduroy dress and a wool sweater to soak in solar rays until I'm warm enough to take the plunge. I've often asked David how he can stand around in a Speedo before and after swimming in cold weather. He says he isn't cold. The bone deep cold I associate with hypothermia sets in fifteen minutes after I get out. A hot shower helps, and warm clothes that hold in body heat. I drink hot tea or eat an apple. Cold isn't an idea. When I dive in it takes me completely — fingertips, toes, chest, arms. The back of my neck is cold. Butch says he doesn't like it when the hairs on his arms freeze. Carolyn wears a fur coat after winter swims, stays out if she thinks her hair is going to freeze. Karen has been known to walk through snow or ice to swim on days it's too slick to drive. Snow swimming occurs in a cloud of steam because the air is colder than the water which is always 68 degrees. It's a layer of silver time some people get addicted to. I like fifties and sun. Dan doesn't care how cold it is. He carries it all day, wears jeans, plaid flannel shirt, down vest. I don't swim every day, I swim when I can stand it. If cold shakes me the way a fever or flu might, I go faster, slap the water with my arms, kick harder. If that doesn't warm me up I get out. One day last winter in a freezing rain, under the gunmetal skies I associate with the Midwest, I found myself at the Springs, this time bundled in down coat, angora hat, fur-lined leather gloves, wool socks and hiking boots. As I walked around the pool, I watched Lori swim in steam, her perfect stroke and fast kick slicing water and cold air. She swam a mile — *down, back, slice, kick, back, down, down, back, slice, kick, back* and out. Skin glowing red and full pregnant belly stretched to round perfection, she was magnificent.

The Universal Deck Change

You should write about the universal deck change, Nathan says. He's wrapped a white towel around him, is peeling off a layer of clothes, sweat pants I think, though I don't look carefully because one doesn't peer about during the universal deck change. Some people are fast and slick about it, others lumpy. We carry on like married couples getting dressed in the morning except no one shows private skin. It's more relaxed than the locker room at a gym or indoor pool where the sexes are segregated, more modest than either bath house where people sun bathe naked, for one thing. I wear a sweatshirt dress and change underneath it, sometimes managing to pull on a pair of sweat pants. In cold weather I use a goofy blue angora hat, wrap up in a towel, throw on a long dress, drop my towel, then peel off the wet swim suit. On cold days the universal deck change is fast. Molly, Eric and Nathan can get jeans on. Some swimmers can get dress clothes on after a lunch hour swim, but can't manage both underwear and pants so they go back to work invisibly half dressed. Eric's deck change is free-wheeling. After he strips out of his speedo, he twirls it with one index finger spraying a wide circle of space and everyone close by. Says, *It keeps my suit from getting moldy*. Recently I watched a morning swimmer take cotton underwear and a bra out of her swim bag, drop them on the deck, pull on a fringed poncho, hook the bra around her waist, pull up the underpants. I asked how she'd get the bra hooked under all those layers and she said as if it were obvious, *I go upstairs to do that!* Most of us don't flash underwear about, though some men will stand around in their jockeys, which cover more skin than a speedo. I went swimming one night in black lycra underwear which covered more of me than lots of bathing suits. It felt light and good to swim like that, close to skinny dipping. Karen peels in and out of shorts and t-shirts and into her suit and vice-versa without missing a beat. We swim, get out of the water, and depending on how cold it is, we dry in the sunlight or wrap a towel around and peel off the wet suit. The key to winter swimming is the universal deck change.

Sweep

Sometimes all I can do is sweep,
sweep dog hair and leaves out of the kitchen,
dust globs out of the hall, shock out of me,
anything out of anywhere.
Sometimes all I can do is sweep.

Sometimes there is so much love
around me, the world is a vast
and brilliant soul, a magnetic thought
through which I fly, clear, wind swept
and true, to you.

How to Swim in a Fjord

for Gen

Don't ask how cold it is until you get out. A warm day helps. Wear something loose so you can change clothes quickly. That's what I thought, but the water is so astounding you don't notice you're wet when you get out, are simply relieved, the way I was the time I died of anaphylactic shock and was brought back by a shot of adrenaline to the heart. Wear swimming shoes because the shoreline is littered with sharp rocks. If bare feet slow you down your legs will grow numb, turn bright red. Look down to find safe footing in ice clear salt water. Knee high is deep enough to swim. Take a full breath (you won't get another for awhile) and dive in. Shout and again shout. People on the shore, who know to stay out of water that is uninhabitable, will clap. Turn over on your back, try to catch your breath. Flip over and try a free style crawl. You'll make four arm strokes, maybe six before it is clear to every cell of you, even your brain, that the water is simply too cold to move through, is stiff. Perhaps you are starting to freeze. Kick. Move as fast as possible back to shore. Belly float, head above water, hand pull yourself from stone to stone. If you stand up, you'll cut your feet. They're numb so it won't hurt until later. Pull yourself onto a boulder and try not to fall over. You will tingle. The sun has not gone down for a month. The rocks are warm. It is the longest day of the year. *Is it cold?* A tall man asks. I look up and again up into his eyes, blue eyes. *How cold is it?* I ask and he laughs, *Ten maybe eleven degrees*, which translates by an odd series of calculations Europeans accomplish quickly, to the low fifties. *Sometimes colder*, he says. His eyes are still laughing. *Now*. I say, *Now it's colder*. I tell him I heard there was a man who swam around the island, covered himself with vaseline to keep in the heat. *Not in a long time*, he says. *That was in the 30s*. The man's name was Sigurd Steverson. He had twin sons, ran movie projectors at the cinema, knew the history of Tromsø, visited the schools, told stories to the children. Now the children learn stories about him.

Jugging

Lately I have been wondering how much water is necessary for the deep emerald color we see from the top of the steps to manifest. The water is clear next to my body, but a few inches away a luscious teal and emerald color wraps seamlessly around the clarity that flows between my fingers or toes. More than a jug, I think, because a jug of water from Barton Springs looks like any other jug of water. Thoreau said Walden Pond was blue, even when it froze. He wrote about a freight train full of blue chunks of ice. I've been wondering what goes on in people's minds when they swim. I asked Scott, who is a lifeguard. He said he'd have to think about it. Barbara thinks about work the first lap, giving anything annoying to the depths. After that she mellows out, finds a rhythm, drifts. Karen goes in and out of thinking about her stroke, then works on problems. I let golden streaks of underwater light clear pain out of me, exalt in the cold charge. Stephen says in chlorine pools he watches people's feet, counts ceramic tiles, recites the alphabet, forwards, backwards, makes lists, works on his speed. At Deep Eddy Pool last Thursday I watched a man swim under water on his back, the way Olympic racers do it. In the ocean Stephen worries about what's underneath him or about keeping his head above the water. In California, near my parent's house, I watch fog roll off the Santa Rosa Mountains while I swim outdoors in a heated pool. I come close to praying while I'm in the water, asking for clarity, for wisdom, less sorrow. Sometimes I can hardly get into the water, but know if I dive in, I'll swim. I'll do a mile, unless it's really cold, then I'll do a half. Once I engage, the body takes over — like sex. One of the guards said after five hundred meters, he hits a rhythm and his mind empties. Scott, who is not a lifeguard, says swimming is as close to mental quiet as he ever gets. He said one coach gave the swim team milk jugs half-full of water instead of kick boards to power up their legs. He found he could do laps almost forever while singing songs to himself consisting of only the word *jug*, called it *jugging*, which is wonderfully idiotic but could be dangerous, I think, like a computer virus, junking up the mind, spamming something useless into every crevice until nothing works. It's probably safer to wonder how much water is necessary for the teal and emerald effect to manifest, or simply let the body take over, though jugging didn't do Scott much harm, now that I think about it, his mind works decently and his legs are strong.

The Final Drift

There is a drift to it,
the final hours.
The spirit spreads out,
touching loved ones,
hovering in threads of light
and soul that knit us
to each other
and when it's done,
the body, incredibly frail, turns
into something foreign.
Some die alone
which is wrong.

There's no path to this place.
We arrive by accident,
cannot tell which
moment will be the last
or know until it occurs,
or know at all.
We're pulled to the riveting
necessity of it,
a grim truth,
the fact of it —
just, unjust,
peaceful, horrendous.
It eats the living
as an afterthought.

Later
the psyche re-arranges —
parts drift to nothingness,
new parts emerge —
so every death, as every
birth, profoundly
changes the essence of
everyone it touches.
Some go sweetly, like robins.

We become small children
who cannot understand,
can only gape,
can only wrap our arms
around our trunks
and rock,
startle at morning light,
at snowfall and star glow,
at an emerald pool,
at each other —

At each other,
at the elemental
veracity of life,
its vibrant
and passionate
contrast
to death's still, all
consuming sweep.
The mystery is dark
the mystery is death
and also it is
life.

About to be a Whole Lot Better

The sky is always there, but it isn't exquisite until Catfish looks up from the water. Once he arrived just before dawn. A horned owl flew across the water, brushing his whiskers with its wings. That was five hundred years ago. My favorite way to see the sky is through water as I curl backwards to the surface out of a back dolphin dive. Nathan said one of the guards had a photograph taken under water of guard stand one — white elevated chair, lopsided umbrella, blue sky, white clouds, blurred and abstract. When I visited Beverly two days before he died, I put my hand over his and said, *I've brought you a touch of the water.* Nathan said when he was working the entrance to the pool he would hear again, again, we still hear it, I said it today, *How are you?* and the response, *About to be a whole lot better.* A cool exhilaration settles into swimmers. On the way in we often hug or touch the arm or hand of someone leaving the way friends and even strangers will touch the stomach of a pregnant woman. Nathan sits cross-legged, face turned to a warm January sun. He's an attorney, worked on a public law suit in Kentucky to get damages for family farmers whose land and relatives were radiated by oil companies. He is linking what he knows about the water to what civil order means. After the doctor told my father he had three months to live, he said, *Do what you've always wanted to do, immediately.* Father did nothing different than he'd done the day before, spent his last days living the life he'd created for himself, raw and unfinished as it was, full of love and imperfection. Recently it occurred to me that it would be all right to stop existing, a relief in fact, but sunlight and shadow on the water were metallic. Green along the shoreline smudged to black, backlit by a blinding winter sun the instant before twilight — *What the hell*, I thought, *I'll stick around, see what the water's like tomorrow.*

Swimming Together

> *Six children from University Junior High School*
> *swim at Barton Springs in the Spring of 1960*

Saundra remembers the occasion more than the swim,
remembers putting her toe into the water, splashing around.
She wanted the event to end.

You could wait forty years to talk to Saundra Kirk.
It would be worth it — rich, searching, complex.
She said she was, and is, an introvert.

New friendships began with the students next to her
in alphabetical order, and Alice Embree — also an introvert,
if you don't count the impact of her politics.

Austin integrated schools from the twelfth grade down, *Stair Step*
Integration. Alice befriended her, made being one of six children
on the *Integration Team* all right.

The school principal initiated the Barton Springs event
by giving his black children the day *off*, or trying to —
the day of the school picnic. The children felt excluded.

Thus began the procession. Six teenagers of color walked down
the wide staircase in 1960 and plunged into the emerald water.
Then they got out.

She remembers cameras, flash bulbs, stories in the newspaper,
but can't find her yearbook, has forgotten one name. *Sandra Anderson*
was there, she says, *and James Means, Lois Lyons, James Glover —*

Her mother bought a pink swim suit and carrying case at
Marie Antoinette's, downtown, on Congress, *One of the first*
clothing stores in Austin where we could purchase—

where we could try on clothes. Saundra's mother was a school

Continued

teacher. Her father was the first Negro to integrate the US
Post Office in Central Texas. He was a Postal Clerk.

She says it was an honor but also overwhelming
to be the token generation. *We moved quickly into the mainstream,
but we were challenged at every level.*

The challenges were profound, and made me cry.
But that's another poem. Bev was Director of Parks
and Recreation then, took the **Black White** signs

out of park facilities, told staff to admit everyone —
before the city asked him to. He was proud of that.
Later, Bev's wife, Lois, was Saundra's English teacher

at Austin High. She remembers Saundra's name forty years
ago was *Vicky. She was the kind of student teachers remember,*
Lois said, *used what she learned immediately, loved new words.*

Today Saundra tells me, *If it had just been a school picnic,
a plunge into the Springs to cool off, perhaps I would have
thought about the beauty of the water.*

*But it was more than that. We were making history.
I went because my mother said to go.
I was the first in line.*

The Garden in the River

When I first came to Barton Springs in the early 70s, we swam above a jungle of underwater flora, duck weed, water lilies, perch, white bass, large mouth bass, Mexican tetra, catfish, minnows, turtles. Underwater colors were crisp. The children found a nest of Mallard eggs alongside the clock pole. Water was so clear it seemed to have no depth. Someone tossed in an Asian grass carp. We called it Big Blue, watched it swirl and flop, particularly in the morning, for several years before the water police realized it could eat the ecosystem. They should have left it. Carp eat algae, algae that blooms up and down local creeks, algae that feeds on fecal runoff from golf courses which use gray water and treated sewage to keep fairways green, algae that comes from over development on the watershed. When the creeks dry up, it hardens like papier mâché, chokes the aquifer. Some algae is natural, but now there is too much. Children throw *Cladophora*, which is a coarse green alga, at each other and wear green beards. *Fissidentales* is muddy moss that grows in miniature forests on top of silt. No one likes it. Globs break loose, string up to the surface, fill our bathing suits with muck and explode in blizzards of particles that turn the water alien. *Calothrix* makes the shallow end slippery. Sometimes we look down on the universe of air bubbles it produces. *Batrachospermum* is red and likes fresh water springs. *Oscillatoria* grows in large sheets on the sides of the pool, like fur. Except for moss, algae and a few spear-leaf plants (*potamogeton*), the bottom of the pool is barren. The spiny plants that manage to survive have algae fur coats. I swim down and clean off a spear each time I pass. Biologists replant but most things get choked out. The water that swirls out of the aquifer is emerald and cold, but full of silt from highway and building projects on the watershed. Swimmers look down on a wasteland. On a Public Radio talk show the other night a caller said indigenous inhabitants of this part of the world also had trouble with developers. He said, *Their solution was to kill them.*

Swimming in Regret

> *Non, rien de rien*
> *Non, je ne regrette rien*
>   Edith Piaf

I am listening to idiotic French tapes
which I can understand, unlike my experience,
when French people talk to each other, to me, or even
to their children.

Je regrette, je ne suis pas Monsieur Clémont.
Je suis somebody else.
No, this is not a clock. It is a window.

It is not yet 2 PM (9 in France) and I have
advertised two cars for sale, interrupted a fight
and read poetry at a television studio.

I would like to have no regrets
but that's not how I feel. It is less that I might have done
things differently, more that too much is lost.

The pool is closed today.
Reflections at the moment are *after* Monet,
Monet on a gray day, Monet in gray.

It is no good to swim in regret.
I do the best I can. If I had acted differently,
I would be someone else.

A grackle walks across the pool steps
carrying a thirty-million-year-old fossil, showing off.
I know this bird.

It would trade the fossil any time
for a granola bar, but I don't have one. Two more birds
fly in loops down to the water tossing, catching —

then dropping a French fry.
Water rings radiate until a gust of wind makes it look
like the creek is flowing backwards.

I know which way the water flows.
I know who is here and who is not. We make choices,
live apart from those who would have it that way.

Are you Japanese?
Non, je ne suis pas japonaise. Je suis an American woman,
a poet, a mother.

I am listening to nonsense in French
to hold off loss that is too great. *Are 2 + 2 Seven?*
Unlike most of what is wrong —

These errors are not difficult to catch.

Floating in Traffic

I'm riding the Airport Express to San Francisco. As I get on the bus a woman says, *Fish are spawning*. We ride to Petaluma which used to be the chicken capital of the world, but now it's not. The bus driver's name is Mark. He was a surfer. I say, *I don't get how people stand up on those things*. He says, *The waves hold you up. You swim out and catch a wave, lean into the motion, become part of it*. I'm doubtful. He drives a bus, but used to work on a chicken farm. There is a poem here. My powerbook is held together with packing tape, but it works. We are floating through traffic. Four lanes move nicely to Marin, vultures circle the overpass at San Rafael. Mark says to expect slow progress in the Navato Narrows, a two lane highway gorge that flows between rolling hills and fog banks. A few days ago I was in Los Angeles, sailing on the Santa Monica Freeway, before that Houston, before that London where they go backwards. Mark tells passengers how to check into flights, how to catch the bus back up to Santa Rosa next week. I've been riding the Airport Express for twenty years. One of my favorite drivers is Claire. She talks a blue streak and her voice is cheery, says, *If you liked the ride my name is Claire, if you didn't my name is Betty*. Claire says passengers bring her stories from all over the world. I ask Mark if he knows Shirley, another driver who chats with everyone on the bus. Mark says she is his *little blueberry muffin*. He stops in San Rafael, tells us to welcome new passengers onto the bus, says it is our bus now, relinquishes control quickly, must be a happy person. Says he read a poem about water at a poetry reading in Santa Monica. The Golden Gate Bridge is beautiful but the name is misleading. It's a bridge, not a gate and it's red, not gold. Golden Gate is what they call the harbor. A woman next to me is crying. Her parents have died and she's been clearing out the house in Santa Rosa. Her cousin jumped off the bridge. She says it was five years before she could cross it again. Mark says to take a deep breath. When she does he says it makes him feel better too.

Swimming in Karma

Cherokee said perhaps I had a Karmic debt
to pay to the dream that slashed me neck to foot,
one side of my body laid open.

Even though someone had thought to apply scotch tape,
a transparent gesture to be sure, rawness glistened
in midday sun.

What is the currency? How does one pay a karmic debt?
Barbara thought tears were the currency. I've thought recently
it would help to cry.

I am too angry. Kathleen told me a long time ago she
thought I was mad at God, which is true but pointless since I
have no idea what *God* means.

I suspect life is the essential miracle of the universe, not what
religions say about one god or another. I'm not sure I owe
anything to people who rip me apart.

The question then, water blowing gray and soft against itself
as I sit alongside the pool trying to stop being angry,
the question is, why do I think I owe them anything at all?

And the answer has to be that somewhere inside me
is a child who feels guilty for not being dead. Cherokee
finds things out because if you leave a sentence hanging —

He waits a long time and then asks you to complete
the thought. It's not possible to lie to him. I told him
the dream because he asked why —

I was staring, staring into the water and he said, *That's a
serious injury. I suggest you avoid those people.*
Which I have done.

But today I find myself telling him it was a bad idea to dive

Continued

into the dream, too much pain in it.
He says you go back to see how much you've changed.

He said he was able to make peace with his father not because
his father changed, but because he did. I was curious.
Now I'm not. Now I am exhausted.

I asked him how I'd know when the debt had been paid.
He said I'd know.

I Like to Think of Father

Anytime I don't know what to do, feel lonely, or need to laugh I like to think of Father. He is any age — white flowing hair just before he died, light around him, or the tall young man whose intellect and zany sense of humor astonished everyone. Sometimes I think of him in the swimming pool, long legs, pot belly, smoke from the grill wafting above California smog. I like to think of Father reading poetry — the phrasing, how he found the finest, most intelligent, ironic twist in anything. I like to think what he would do sometimes when I am in situations he would not condone. *What now?* I ask him. And I laugh. He held himself to a tight leash. I like to think about the house on Longview Street, how angry I was at him when I needed someone to fight. He stood by me no matter how dumb a thing I'd done, or wrong. I like to think of Father scowling when he was annoyed. I like to think of him looking out the window, off into clouds, through reality into some idea that held his attention when we could not. Now that he's gone, I sometimes ask Helen what to do when my son acts up. *Cut him some slack*, she said recently. *Remember what you were like*. I found a letter from my father's brother in which I was referred to as *the problem child in every family*, suggesting punishments my parents ignored. When I arrived in Los Angeles from Winter in Connecticut, father heated the pool so we could swim, fed us steak and Bristol Cream Sherry on the rocks to celebrate, no matter what time of day or night it was. I like to think of Father reading because it brought him peace. I like to think about the way his intellect surrounded me, as if I were an island in the ocean of all he knew. I remember that he waited patiently for me to grow up, and just before he died, told me I'd have to do it soon.

Everything Wrong and Broken

Everything wrong and broken
is tangled up together
in a knot of debris
that floats down the swollen
river of my soul
and out, and out.

I race to hold it back.

Something of value is hidden
in the mess,
something of me I cannot
do without,
the beloved, for instance,
but the river has it,
I do not —
can only flood
or lose myself,
until what's left is
scoured empty and raw
or on the other hand,
clear.

Everything wrong and broken
swept away —
a new day, stark
and brave.

Something's bound to happen
once I forgive reality
for not containing you.

A Question of Degree

The temperature at my mother's house creeps up and up. She is collecting degrees to warm her against death's cold breath, is always cold when I am boiling in my skin, wears long underwear, wool pants, sweaters and a coat when I am content with just long pants, closed shoes, a jersey, and a sweater. The pool where Mother lives is hot and small. Lelia invites me to come swimming but Mother says the residents get out when I swim. It is a therapeutic pool. Across the street is a huge lake I could walk around but there is no time. I itch to swim in cold water, go for a walk in San Francisco. Ed says swimming a mile a day will make me live to be a hundred. I think of the poems Stanley Kunitz has written since he turned 90, of the baby Heather is carrying as we walk uphill. If I lived here, I would grow accustomed to these hills. Dr. Liz says she numbs out, tells herself to put one foot in front of the other when she walks uphill, uphill, uphill to her house in the Castro. I like the way climbing makes my legs feel, but I don't see how people do it and talk at the same time. She rides her bike downhill to work at Kaizer and uphill, uphill, uphill to get back home. I'm proud of Liz, her life and work, and I love her. She's happy here. San Francisco is an aerobic city. This afternoon I found a grass path at the edge of a high cliff overlooking Goat Rock Beach. I stood in a soft breeze above an ocean made entirely of waves of foam, white and then soft blue, sweet wind. I have no use for pools. David said the physiology of cold water swimmers changes so they don't get hypothermia. Corpuscles in the skin stop collecting blood in cold water, so the body doesn't lose the heat it needs to stay alive. Our bodies stop putting energy where it will hurt us the way they help us separate from people or conditions that annihilate the heart. Small red angels protect people crazy enough to swim in fifty degree salt water, small angels dive below the surface of their skin, hoard degrees of warmth, hold off Death's cold breath the way mother keeps turning up the heat. Every year it gets hotter in her living room.

Emerald

I met Esmeralda
at the pool today,
cupped my hands
to bring her water
from the spring.

She's two weeks old,
swaddled in soft cotton,
arms stretching
in a velvet,
warm breeze
beneath the old pecan tree.

Karen, Francisco, Jo, Barbara
and I each dab water
on her feet, knees, forehead—
a first of many baptisms.

When I ask Frank what
it's like to have two children,
he replies,
More than twice the joy.

Drowning in Teachers

The pool is closed because four inches of rain have washed too much urban runoff into the water, too much animal and human sewage, lawn fertilizer, so I attend a teacher's conference. It is difficult to get in. An official glowers when I ask for the program. Possibly she wants to protect me from the content: *The Literary Canon as a Living Document, Make Mine Music — The Mozart Effect is just the tip of the iceberg . . . Blast off to Literacy.* I am listening to a teacher say she will not *spoon feed* black literature to black students. I say, *Why the hell not?* Mother tried to teach me to bite my tongue when I become aggressive. Father suggested I do school *puzzles* in class and then read my own books until they let me out. I would rather be swimming but the water is polluted. Strategies for making washed out content palatable to stoned out teenagers with ambitious parents wear me out. I find the book exhibit. In one text book I read (in about three seconds) about the plague in Europe, Queen Elizabeth, and Edmund Spenser. I see a map (too small to read) of the known world in the 16th century, and a long text bar announcing the educational objectives this material addresses — the methodology of the sound bite applied to the mind, hundreds of books, pamphlets, historical documents, primary material condensed to a slick book one inch thick, each page divided into blocks like a newspaper. The teacher's guide is slightly more interesting, but they don't provide these to children because it would cause them to know answers to preset questions prematurely. Text book committees decide what books can be used in Texas classrooms. We achieve these graphically interesting but ignorant products by applying the methodology of the market place and political regulation to public education, which is neither a business nor an elected office. It ought to be a service. I am drowning in teachers and in the books they are mandated to use. I hear an old friend's cheery voice and think if there are a few good teachers, something will be salvaged, but I am still drowning, drowning in teachers and suffocated by their books.

"Self Portrait Blowing Bubbles" by Susan Bright

Swimming in Flowers

Do not stand by my grave and weep.
I am not there, I do not sleep.

I remembered the first few words. Helen sent it to us when my father died. Until today, I never knew who wrote it. I was getting ready to go to the pool for Beverly's service. He gave me the poem, along with other things over the years, to read for him *sometime*. Georgeane and Tibb organized a poolside memorial on what would have been his 87th birthday.

I am a thousand winds that blow.
I am the diamond glint on snow.

I couldn't find the file. Three days ago I pulled it from one of my cabinets when I was looking for something else, automobile repair records. I called Hellie who lives in upstate New York. She's a musician. They remember things. I asked her how she was and she said, *Terrible*. She'd fallen last week. Helen is 91, has had four hip operations. *I hurt everything except my nose*, she said. *How'd you miss that?* I asked her and she said she wasn't sure. I said I was looking for a poem. She began to recite it. I said, *That's amazing*, which made her forget the rest. I told her I needed it in ten minutes. *Give me a lot of notice, why don't you?* she said, after her housekeeper found it by following instructions like, *I put it in that old blue bowling bag along with other things I want to keep. Look in the zipper compartment.* In her defense, I don't believe Helen ever went bowling in her life. She was and is enthralled with music and with us. She was also a swimmer. She read the rest of the poem to me:

I am the sunlight on ripened grain.
I am the gentle autumn rain.
When you wake in the morning hush
I am the swift uplifting rush
of quiet birds in circling flight.
I am the soft starlight at night.

I typed as she read. Hellie said the author was Joyce Fossen. I thanked her, as I do daily whether I speak to her or not, because she took care of me when I was an infant, while my brother was dying, and loved me, because she showed me how to be an artist, the daily work, the truth and joy of it. When I got to the pool, Lois, Tibb, Georgeane, Marilyn and a few other people were there. I was telling Georgeane that Bev had given me a poem to read, years ago, just as Lois pulled a copy of it out of her purse and asked Georgeane to have someone read it. I read it along with two of Bev's own poems, which he sent to me last summer on my birthday. He didn't know it was my birthday. It was my favorite gift. I don't think I ever saw Bev that there wasn't a gift in it. Tibb played *Home Sweet Home* on the harmonica, blowing back at a rough March wind that kept storm clouds across the river from darkening our ceremony. Eric read water passages from the I-Ching. Marshall brought a photograph of a young Bev on a bucking horse, related Bev's advice to boys. *Don't wait to be a great man. Be a great boy.* Twenty or so swimmers gathered. Tom took a panoramic photograph with a small camera that turned around in a circle. He ran to one end of our group to get in the final revolution. We floated flowers on the water. Lois tossed in the largest long stemmed rose I've ever seen. Red petals became soft sails. We threw in orchids and carnations, ferns and baby's breath. It was Francisco's third birthday. As we posed for Tom's photo, we were singing happy birthday to Bev and to Francisco. The swimmers swam a lap for Beverly, together, marveling at the beauty of the day. Gary was the first one in. He held a cluster of yellow roses in his teeth, wore day glow Mardi Gras beads around his neck. We swam through flowers. When we got out they began to cluster, but not downstream where you'd expect them to go. They swirled back to the place where the springs come out, back to the source — and circled there reminding us of the twirling miracle we all seem to be.

Do not stand by my grave and weep.
I am not there. I do not sleep.

A Thick Layer of Time

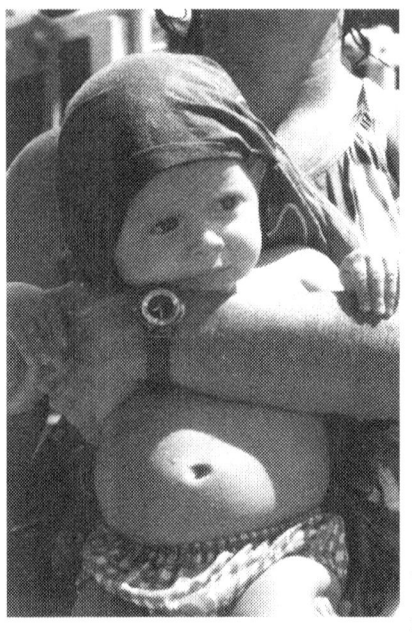

We are swimming in a thick layer of time. Its cold, emerald force parts as we pull against the current, adds to our momentum when we move steadily downstream. Today the journey centers on the fat bulb of an infant's belly, how she cracks up if we make gurgling baby sounds. We celebrate the nubs of new teeth bursting out of perfect gums, two small arcs of innocence, that fill up tooth by tooth until there is a whole mouth full and she goes off to college. I am mesmerized by infants, how they complete the circle of a woman's time. To see fathers nurture babies, gives me hope. Once swimming in the thick of time, I stepped dripping wet out of the river that never stops changing into a universe composed entirely of me, knew right from wrong, how everyone should change, provided time tables, checked everyone's progress. I searched the shallows, memorized patterns of light caught in my shadow, swam through schools of fish, duck weed. Underwater gardens full of turtles, crawfish, snails — flourished beneath me as I swam above, kicking steadily, breathing a perfect song of self, searching the river of the soul for an essential matrix, compelling beyond what I could dream. But my significance slipped away, made a gurgling creek sound as it spilled past one outstretched, cupped hand after another. Often in a time I didn't see coming, the way a swimmer falls into perfection, kicking, breathing, arms pulling at the sky, oblivious to external reality, the way suddenly a child is grown up and gone, before we remember to enjoy the small miracle of him, of her, often in the kind of time that presents itself before we think to ask, I have stepped out of the river to a place so desolate I can't move. Father is gone, Mother is old, I've lost perfection to a distant layer of time. People haggle over art, saying, *This is mine, you can't look at it unless you give me something — money, fame, something to believe in, forget it, just give me money.* Sometimes I step out, legs trembling to the pull of gravity, feet and hips too stiff to function out of water and I feel my own death, fall at it the way I run into everything I've done wrong, find comfort in the granular mass of it even though it's pointless and not what I want. At times like that I get back in the water, step out someplace else. This morning I held baby Esmeralda in my arms but facing out, so she could see light playing between the shade of pecan leaves on the water. I kissed the back of her small baby head that can just hold itself up and watched light ripple on the water just past her tiny shoulder. She watched the water a long time, filling her new soul with its dance, with the brush of velvet air on skin. She doesn't know it's separate from her in any way. Perhaps it's not.

"Cape Girl," photo by Jo Bellonci. (Esmeralda in her mother's arms)

Swimming in Grief

Comfort,
and be comforted, Brian tells me
as I leave for Benjamin's
memorial —
suicide after a long
struggle with addiction.

His mother is a poet,
and a swimmer.
His sister was one
of our guards.

I want to hit the priest
with a pea shooter
until
he stops reciting dogma.

And then his words
fill my chest with so much
pain, I can hardly
breathe.

You can't prepare
for this, Robin tells me
afterwards,
It's worse than
we can possibly imagine.

Eclipse Party

When it slides into a full eclipse, when the shadow of our spinning planet falls across the moon, is the shadow also spinning? Ten years ago I stayed up all night to send toxic energy out through the slit of a lunar eclipse — to nothing, or maybe to something we don't understand. I didn't swim. The temperature dropped fifty degrees since yesterday and I grew cold, head tilted back to watch the moon unhinge. A small circle of swimmers dove through teal blue water as the last rib of light went out. A howling flew up when the *red shade* descended, which is actually red brown, like blood in water. Eggs twirl through me, swim out in a thick, clear yoke. David brought a telescope, demanded to be told which way was north. People pointed in various directions. Helga brought hot basil tea spiked with vodka which was delicious. Helga is interesting. Just when you think she's one thing, she becomes something else. Mary roasted pecans in sugared egg whites. Marilyn brought brie and hummus, and the wise grace she gives us. Karen and Arye appeared with a large tray of vegetables, and goodwill. Mara told about the Russian poet, Konstantin, who lived in our wide heat as long as he could stand it. She took a photograph of Grady slipping a German Luger away from him at a poetry reading. Mara visited him in a tilted cabin on the side of a mountain in Pennsylvania, manuscripts piled high alongside a wood burning stove. She was afraid the cabin would roll over and ignite. When I met Konstantin he was writing in pieces of twelve languages, a poet exiled from his native voice. Gus got in the water for the first time in winter. Helga swam along with Mary and Mary's granddaughter. Four generations of women in Mary's family swim here — Mary, Ginny, Beth and Kaya. Tonight so much slipped past the moon I echo and cringe. Sometimes, when I think I can't go on another minute, things turn. It's usually because I've forgotten something. Tonight we gathered by the water to watch a full lunar eclipse, something beautiful and holy obscured, a hushed symphony of chatter, a cellular howl, the ebb and flow of us.

Elephant Buddha

First there were photographs
in exquisite color.
You could identify an eye,
part of the trunk.
The last one revealed the whole thing —
a mountain in the shape of an elephant
which, I discovered,
was the horizon,
a huge mountain shaped like
an elephant, a dream
of the Elephant Buddha.

It was nearly a planet —
serene, green, a mountain of rock,
trees, streams, lakes, alpine flowers,
breathtaking waterfalls
showering a huge soul.

A national park spread
across its skull.
There were highway signs to it,
and books in which houses
were painted upside down.
Three of my favorite activists
were selling
placards along the road.

I just looked and celebrated,
celebrated and looked, looked
at the Elephant Buddha—
fluid, joyful and erotic.

Swimming in Hearings

I trick myself into thinking I won't stay long, but I do. I speak before the Environmental Protection Agency against re-opening a fifty-year-old pipeline. An Exxon affiliate wants to run gasoline through it, uphill from Houston to El Paso, under pressure, the kind of process that created a mile wide fire ball in Bellingham, WA, killing three children. Elected officials speak first. Three of five are friends of mine. They are against it, which is encouraging. Mothers point to schools 100 feet from the pipeline, which also runs above ground across a creek where flashfloods can be counted on to rip it apart, poisoning the aquifer that supplies San Antonio, San Marcos and Austin. Nineteen oil leaks have occurred in the last twenty-five years, one every 15.5 months. The leaders in the industry are forming international committees to protect the environment. Solar energy makes sense, or wind. It's good business to protect the environment because we live here, but Longhorn doesn't get it. They hire experts from central casting who read scripts. I've skipped dinner and begin to float into a low blood sugar drift, but manage to stay until it's my turn to speak. Then I swim out, picking up the address for written comments as I go. The Environmental Protection Agency could shut this down, but there is powerful lobbying for it. Longhorn is trying to unload outmoded technology in the hinterland. Maybe they will get away with it, blow up a few intersections, a school or two. There will be public outrage. Exxon will sell Longhorn in an afternoon, go into wind energy and solar power. I wonder if our great-grand-children will have time to learn to read before the planet is irrevocably poisoned.

I know how to swim in moonlight alone

avoiding the sleek eel that lives
in a crevice along one side of the far edge
of the pool.

I know how to look through deep
green-black water and see nothing
and accept it.

I trust moonlight
to blast through my dark hollows —
find something pure.

I know how it feels to stretch
into cold knowing, to roll with a fat
moon, hope for nothing.

I know how to send you off
and not care if you understand.
I've watched elliptical spotlights dance

on black tuxedo water, have watched fireworks
explode while I float belly up like a penguin
dressed in moonlit skin and sequins.

I know how to swim in moonlight alone
and not call out a name —
not be a hollow gong.

I'm strong and I float which
does not mean I don't also know to howl
at the white globe, or engage

the ones who swirl into my drift —
but in the moonlight, no one is here
and I know how to swim alone.

The River Needs a Friend

I ache to swim but every time I go back I get sick. I go anyway. As long as the water is there I will adapt. I get off a plane in a dark mood. Brigid Shea is on the airport television talking about Save Our Springs. I love Austin. Shudde Fath has found the names of everyone who spoke at the Barton Springs Revolution, an all-night city council hearing on June 7, 1990 to stop development on the aquifer. Tonight's the ten-year anniversary. There's an award ceremony in an hour. I'll be late. It was a decade of hearings, demonstrations, hard work — Earth First, Sierra Club, Greenpeace, Save Barton Creek Association, the Audubon Society, neighborhood associations, civic groups, people of all ages gathered into a movement. Our victories were short lived. There were ordinances and elections, hard won but eventually discouraging. We began to fight among ourselves. Developers bought votes, legislative committees and agencies, sold their projects and moved on. When I go back to the Midwest, I appreciate the necessity of what we've tried to do here, even though it hasn't really worked, even though the water quality is terrible compared to what it was ten years ago. My hometown on Lake Michigan has three Superfund clean-up sites. There is a mountain of asbestos on the lake, a tannery next to an old electric plant that periodically spews out PCBs, a jet fuel dump that leaches poison into the largest inland water system in the world. Threadgills fills up with people I am proud to know. Eddie Wilson is feeding Austin activists again. Bill Oliver arrives to sing the songs that make us love him, tight lyrics, environmental sense, satire. He's come from a service for Glen Allyn who was killed with his daughter in a car wreck. In 1968 Bill and Glen floated down the Mississippi River on a raft. Glen stepped ashore to call home and found out he'd been drafted. Bill is late, the crowd has thinned. His energy is vibrant and professional, funny and good because that is how we do it here. You go from personal loss back to the movement. The work goes on. If we keep singing, if we keep working, our hearts won't break. An official who was one of us at the Barton Springs Revolution is fighting with a eco-activist who has (or hasn't) threatened to throw a pie in someone's face. I try to make peace between them. It is a mistake. I've been out of touch and don't know who is right. There are disputes here, but also a common focus. Bill is singing, which makes me cry because I know the raw necessity it comes from. He is singing *The River Needs a Friend*.

Swimming with Rick

Today Rick got back in the water. He's been sick and no one knows what's wrong, reminding me of Pete, who I used to call the swimming god. Like Pete, Rick's illness began with loss of muscle control and exhaustion. Both were athletes, long distance swimmers, cyclists. Both were in perfect physical condition when they got sick. Pete, at the worst, had to use a walker. He lost his house, job, went to specialist after specialist and finally got better. But he stopped swimming at Barton Springs because he thought the water made him sick. Rick thought pollution might have caused his illness, or stress. He worked as an x-ray technologist forty hours in three days, then took off the rest of the week. *Taking off* for Rick meant riding seventy-five miles or swimming hard. He stands on the second step, talks about Tassajara, a Zen Monastery near Carmel where he went to understand how to live with illness. He listens to the radio, says my poems make him feel less alone, says he's adapting to limits, wants to see the book when I am done. It will be hard to complete. The river doesn't end, or will it? I hear death in her voice sometimes. The springs are pumping at one fourth normal volume. Rick says swimming could overstress his nervous system, make him worse, but swims anyhow, says there have been gifts in his illness. *When you think everything is all right the universe throws something at you, as if to say — See how you like this!* We laugh, reminding me I need to get my sense of humor back. I consider asking the guard to keep an eye on Rick since I have to leave, but don't. Sick and exhausted, he's is a stronger swimmer than all but one other person in the pool. I think how light we are in water and graceful, how the cold of it evens out pain, how we come back again and again, no matter what. I wonder if it is poisoning us — sores that don't heal, ear infections, sinus problems, intestinal problems, eye infections. I'll be one of the last ones to get out. Dozens of springs used to feed the San Antonio River. Two remain. San Pedro Springs, which ran like Barton Springs, is gone. Last week Cypress Springs stopped running, which dried up Blue Hole in Wimberly. I have a photograph Peach took of a whole Montessori class perched in the diving tree just before they leaped into Blue Hole. My son's arm was in a cast. In the last century, one-fifth of all deaths were caused by bad water. Epidemics raged downstream from town to town. Rick says a good thing about not knowing what is wrong is there is no reason to assume it won't get better.

Parkside Community School Junior High class at Blue Hole, "Ritual of Spring" by Peach Reynolds.

Bodycount

      for Sally Jacques

Honor the way Sally weaves the threads of us
into a whole, creating, alongside the pool,
December first, and again the next December first,
a gathering of art and dance, water and light.

Bring blankets, sit outdoors in the cold night air,
know Tina will sing, know the dance
will give us hope —
at least respite.

Mourn our loved ones lost to AIDS.
Celebrate the ones who endure proving
that the person is greater than the disease.

Sally knows the choreography of this place,
the living sculpture of our time on Earth.

We are all
in the dance.

Myth of Proportion

And snakes are only rivers, sealed up rivers that slide along,
self-contained, like truth, where everything is red clay,
or desert. And moisture exposed to air will vanish
into hot light or be sucked up by grain the way
the Colorado River never makes it to the sea
because of Hoover Dam—named after the man
Very-Old-Grandmother said was the dumbest person
who ever lived, because he ordered farmers to gas torch
cattle, not for supper, but to drive up the price of grain,
during the Depression, when people were starving.
And the red canyons that grew into Lake Mead gleam
like Depression glass when you look down from clouds.
And arroyos feather out like crystals in time
the way large and small reverse themselves. And Sky
is full of holes that are invisible but shake up everything
that passes through them. And time is an invention
that keeps everything from happening at once.
And reality is the Snake that ate a river.
And we are the Snake.

Urban Drift

The first time I saw Vermont Avenue it was boarded up, summer, just after the Watts riots, police on every corner, newspapers blowing in hot air that was toxic. I was working at the USC Law Library. Now Vermont Avenue is Korean, more accurately, several Asian cultures, storefronts in languages I don't understand, which makes me feel small, but is compell-ing the way anything I don't know attracts me. I am on Vermont Avenue because I refuse to negotiate a downtown traffic knot four tiers deep which threads every freeway in LA to every other one. I don't want a random destination, Cleveland or Alaska, for instance. I want to go to USC. I study three maps to get there which takes longer than the drive itself. I am going to visit Dick Drobnick, who I have not seen since I was in high school. Our visit is delightful, an improvement on the time he stabbed the inside of my elbow with a pencil in the third grade possibly (his version of the story) because I was trying to knock him over. Vermont Avenue starts like a placid stream as Vermont Canyon Road winds out of Griffith Park, cuts west through the city and ends at Los Angelos Harbor and the Department of Immigration. It crosses Los Feliz Avenue which runs between Hollywood and Silverlake through the flower filled, old neighborhoods where Eve Caram lives. USC sits primly next to a freeway, is manicured, clear cut from the urban surge around it. I drift past the stretch of Vermont Avenue that was torn up in the 1992 riots, after Rodney King was beaten senseless by LA police. Blacks retaliated by burning Asian businesses which made as much sense as riots ever make, which are reverberations of raw pain. Smog sits on the city like a sullen orange blanket, turning sunlight a strange shade of brown. Cross street names set off memories as my eyes fill up with Asian alph-abets, which tell me Los Angeles has drifted to the Pacific Rim. Meg and I used to drive the fast curves down Sunset Boulevard to the beach before the sun set. My parent's church was on Wilshire Boulevard in Beverly Hills, a fabulously expensive property even then. Father said they should sell the parking lot and do something Christian with the money. I cross Beverly Boulevard which threads to a shopping district where I used to buy buttons from a shop that sold nothing except buttons — buttons made of anything, glitter, gold, plastic, bone, hair, teeth, fake diamonds, diamonds. I'd get discount fabric and make something that started with buttons. I cross numbered street after numbered street. There are signs to Alvarado Street where we used to shop at the Mexican Market, children playing violins, hot food. This time, I step out at USC, leaving Vermont Avenue to the urban flood that threads it through the heart of Watts where violence continues to rip out of the same deep, human rift that rumbled the street the first time I was here.

Swimming in the Beginning

Change so radical it transforms every aspect of our being can only come from people who don't know what they are doing, people free to re-invent the past, present and future as they drift into the thick of it. What if it were illegal to amass great wealth? What if contracts between unequal parties were invalid? Angels toss possibility at the softness of a soul that's open, if only for an instant. An elastic mind can wind its way to possibility, the body follows and then it leads —a twirling dance of life. We are what we do and what occurs because of that, but someone has to say the meaning of it. You can't sort out a single particle of water, map its turbulence, or know in advance how we might fly through time, tumbling like eagles in ecstatic drift. The soul is water leaping off a multifaceted blue cliff. There are people who do not believe in change, who read the present as an extension of what just occurred, thinking us a game of chess, thrilling, complex but immutable. That looks false to me. I have learned to forgive the past for my inability to predict it. I am a swimmer and the water which is my context comes from an explosion in the universe the code of which might add up, or not. Possibly the universe is an improvisation which began by reversing an inward knot of thrust. We can't know why it happened. More likely change is like light, shining in every direction at once, moving in waves that can transform anything, millions of people revising every layer of civilization, for instance. I suspect the potential for radical departure from a world context bent on extinction lies in the clear voices of people who *are* change — even the old woman who practices her death to get it right. Prostrate in a hospital bed she commands the children to hold hands in a circle, says she'll squeeze just before she dies and again when she comes back. It is all right to live and then to die and then to live again. Beginning can start anywhere.

Iris

The vibrance of the universe is so obvious it is difficult to
comprehend what could have led us from wide-eyed knowing
that it is alive.
From nucleus to cell wall is a trillion light years.
The blink of an eye contains the eternal reality of dream. In any tree
there are galaxies with comets flashing through wood like space.
Linear space/time is *A* not *The* dimension.
The translations we are incapable of are more thick than ants.
We can't even talk to fish.
The power to imagine is the power that radiates from star
to planet. I splash water on my face, drops fall on a galactic map
spread out beneath my feet.
Spiral galaxies form with red and living stars ready
to shoot patterns across my skin.
Piles of alphabets, icons, and the love between them
balanced on the rim of a crystal are the images
we have for the bath of universe we move through,
thinking we are earth people,
the illusion of our age,
Earth People,
soon to be condensed,
soon to be transformed.

Our children will wander space like we roamed creekbeds, stones
through our fingers: stars through theirs.
They will sleep, like we do, but with respect for both sides of
the veil.

Swimming in Choice

Autumn Equinox
appeared
and passed as I held
Esmeralda up to the light
which made her
laugh, then vowel talk
to a community
of swimmers
who were conversing
too
in modulating waves
which are
my favorite
orchestra.

Alyce has
a photograph from
1976,
her round belly
ripening
alongside the spring
in August light,
said
chilling beside
the pool was the best time
of her pregnancies,
a community of
mothers,
feet dangling
in an emerald
spring.

Alyce and
I are the first
generation of women
to have a choice

Continued

about fertility.
We grabbed
a slice of time,
laid in a strategy
for balance
that is changing every
aspect of culture,
which was our intent.

We were outrageous
and determined.
Our mother souls
were shattered
by a violent century,
uneven
with its tangle
of evolved men
and
atrocity,
strong women
and misogyny.
The family broke,
and needed to.
The next ones
will be better.

Alyce and I
are war torn,
so it is easy to forget
the obvious —
this ripening,
the joyful laugh of it,
water breaking.
The pull to birth
is essential
to woman's nature
and the key
to every kind

of balance.

I am
happiest
when there
are babies
at hand.

They fill
my soul
and
quiet
the chaos
of my life.

Time flows
to the best of me,
when
I remember
to hold babies up
to
the light.

Going Back for More

Like spent lovers we go back for more, knowing it won't taste as good, driven to touch emerald clarity once more before we plunge back to the day, or night. Yesterday Georgeane stood on the second step, water lapping about her feet. She was wearing a Guatemalan dress, her long athletic body restless as it always looks in street clothes, said she got cold swimming to the dam, had to take a hot shower. It's August. The temperature leveled down to the 90s. Yesterday a gulf storm brought the first clouds in weeks, and seven raindrops. A blast of ozone filled the air with the smell of rain thumping hot earth. It's hard to say how we know one thing from another — attraction from distraction, summer from fall, falling from the dive that is a human life. It seems cooler to me this morning. The old dog slept outdoors last night instead of under the coldest air conditioning vent, in the hallway, next to the bathroom door where everyone trips over him. Outdoor cats are moving. I reach for a sky blue Speedo cap left over from last winter and think, *Not yet, but soon.* Soon enough I'll pull out the gray wool sweater I bought in Wisconsin on a warm autumn day that seemed cold to me, wondering if I'd need more of them, or just this one to hold off hypothermia after swimming in the winter. One was enough. I considered moving back, grew up in those cold northern winters. We had closets inside closets, full of wool skirts, sweaters, slacks, coats, hats, boots, long underwear and face masks. I hated the itch of wool, the mothball smell of closets, but liked the hang of knit on a man's shoulders, the feel of it holding warmth next to my body. I stood on a high bluff above Lake Michigan early mornings waiting for the bus, wind cold knives frantic for my heat, was young, didn't know better, couldn't imagine a place where one could swim outdoors in January in water that is always 68 degrees. Ellen goes back for seconds even in the winter. So does Jim. Even in August the water chills me perfectly, afterwards the air tingles on my skin, welcoming me back to a second native matrix, reminding me that we can change dramatically the overwhelming oppression of scorched light, broken intent, arthritic joints by simply diving into Barton Springs, by lingering in the afterglow, by going back for seconds, more, life force, always more.

About the Poet

Self Portrait with mask, by SusanBright.

Susan Bright is the author of eighteen books of poetry, three of which (*Far Side of the Word*, *Tirades And Evidence Of Grace* and *House of the Mother*) have been recipients of Austin Book Awards. *Tirades And Evidence Of Grace* also won the Violet Crown Award. She is the editor of Plain View Press which has published one-hundred-and-fifty books. Her work as a poet, publisher, activist and educator has taken her all over the United States and abroad. In Texas she has received a proclamation from the Senate honoring her literary and community work, and in Austin she received the Woman of the Year Award in 1990 from the Women's Political Caucus. She is a year around lap swimmer at Barton Springs Pool in Austin, Texas.

About the Artist

Brian Michael Pion is the son and grandson of landscape architects. In his mid-twenties he faced several personal crises for which he turned to meditation. From the meditation came the inspiration to draw and sculpt. His work then evolved to a combination of the two mediums, integrating brilliant color schemes, ordinary geometric patterns and inner meditative visions. The cover piece was created specifically for this collection of poetry.

Photo by Susan Bright

www.ingramcontent.com/pod-product-compliance
Lightning Source LLC
Chambersburg PA
CBHW071022080526
44587CB00015B/2460